Fearless Investing Series: Mutual Funds Workbook **1** 2 3

Find the Right Mutual Funds

Published by John Wiley & Sons, Inc., Hoboken, New Jersey.
Published simultaneously in Canada.

For general information about our other products and services, please contact our Customer Care Department within the United States at 800-762-2974, outside the United States at 317-572-3993 or fax 317-572-4002.

Wiley also publishes its books in a variety of electronic formats. Some content that appears in print may not be available in electronic books. For more information about Wiley products, visit our Web site at www.wiley.com.

ISBN 0-471-71185-3

Printed in the United States of America
10 9 8 7 6 5 4 3 2 1

Introduction

In the 1990s, it seemed that anyone could pick a strong-performing mutual fund and assemble a winning portfolio. With the tailwind of a buoyant market helping them, even relatively poor funds were able to score robust gains.

The past five years, however, have proved far more challenging for investors. Following a brutal bear market from 2000 through early 2003, the industry became engulfed in scandal, dogged by allegations of improper trading and unscrupulous sales practices.

Amid that backdrop, however, investors' faith in mutual funds as a fundamentally sound investment vehicle hasn't been shaken. Investors sent nearly $400 billion to mutual funds in 2003 and 2004. In so doing, they acknowledged that funds, with their built-in diversification and professional management, remain the best way for individuals to build long-term wealth.

We at Morningstar certainly believe that to be true. The year 2004 marked our company's 20th anniversary of providing investors with the information they need to make sound financial decisions. Along the way, we've talked to scores of investors who, empowered by Morningstar's objective research and analysis, have used mutual funds to achieve goals big and small: sending kids to college, remodeling houses, and enjoying worry-free retirements.

Helping even more investors reach their goals was the impetus behind Morningstar's new Fearless Investing Series. The series, as its name suggests, is designed to demystify the often-complex world of investing—and even make it fun. In addition to grounding you, the investor, in the basics of mutual funds, our interactive workbook series gives you concrete advice for selecting the best funds for you and putting the pieces together into a portfolio that delivers maximum long-term returns.

Although the books are sold individually, the three workbooks in the series are designed to be used in conjunction with one another. Book One, *Find the Right Mutual Funds*, provides an overview of how mutual funds work, as well as a discussion of how to evaluate a fund's manager, portfolio, risk/return potential, costs, and tax efficiency. Book Two, *Diversify Your Fund Portfolio*, discusses the keys to building a diversified, all-weather portfolio and gives you concrete pointers for selecting both bond and international funds. The series culminates with Book Three, *Maximize Your Fund Returns*. In this book, you'll find advanced strategies for maximizing your portfolio's return, along with our best tips for bear-proofing your portfolio and knowing when to sell.

Within each workbook, you'll find that we've divided each lesson into four distinct sections: the lesson itself, Fearless Facts, a quiz, and a worksheet. Each workbook also includes an Investing Terms section, a list of additional Morningstar resources, and a Recommended Reading section. Read on for details about how to get the most out of each section.

Lessons: The lessons are designed to give you an overview of a particular topic, along with plenty of real-life examples and concrete tips for putting the knowledge to work in your portfolio.

Fearless Facts: These scannable lists provide you with a quick overview of the key points from the lesson. Use our Fearless Facts to brush up on what you've just learned.

Quizzes: The quizzes help ensure that you've mastered the key concepts in the lesson. You'll find answers for each of the quizzes at the back of each book.

Worksheets: The worksheets are designed to help you put the key concepts in each lesson into practice. You'll find that many of the worksheets ask you to find facts about your own funds and portfolio; the goal of these exercises is to help you understand what you own and to ensure that your portfolio suits your goals and risk tolerance.

Investing Terms: Although Morningstar's Fearless Investing Series assumes that readers do not have any background in finance or investments and thus explains any term mentioned in the text, you can look to the Investing Terms section for a more in-depth definition of each term used in the series.

Additional Morningstar Resources: Morningstar's Fearless Investing Series is designed as an introduction to Morningstar's approach to selecting mutual funds and building portfolios. Investors interested in learning more about Morningstar's other products should consult this list.

Recommended Reading: This is a list of some of Morningstar's favorite books about mutual funds and investing.

Whether you're a novice investor or a seasoned hand looking to maximize your portfolio, we trust that you'll find Morningstar's Fearless Investing Series to be a practical and profitable way to learn about mutual funds and meet your financial goals. We wish you luck on your journey.

Acknowledgments

A number of individuals played a significant role in the production of the Fearless Investing Series. Susan Dziubinski, Peter Di Teresa, and David Harrell, all of whom have a special talent for putting complex topics into easy-to-understand terms, developed most of the lessons that form the basis of the three books in the series. Scott Berry, Christopher Traulsen, Andrew Gogerty, Russel Kinnel, Kunal Kapoor, and Joseph Nasr also contributed valuable content to the series. Morningstar's copy-editing staff, including Elizabeth Bushman and Jason Stipp, worked hard to ensure that the concepts in the book would be clear to novice investors.

Alla Spivak and Erica Moor shepherded the books through the publishing process, coordinating the work of all of the contributors. Morningstar's design staff, notably Lisa Lindsay, Minwha Kim, David Silva, and David Williams, developed the books' design. David Pugh, our editor at John Wiley & Sons, gave us valuable guidance for completing this book.

We also owe a huge debt of gratitude to Catherine Odelbo for helping develop the series' concept and for encouraging Morningstar's analysts to create the best possible products for investors of all experience levels. As head of Morningstar's retail business unit, she has been central to putting Morningstar's motto of "Investors First" into action.

Finally, we're grateful to Morningstar founder Joe Mansueto, who founded this company on the principle that all investors are entitled to high-quality independent investment information. His company has grown by leaps and bounds since Joe founded it 20 years ago, but Morningstar has never deviated from that central principle.

Contents

Know the Ins and Outs of Mutual Funds

Lesson 101: What is a Mutual Fund?

Buying a mutual fund is a lot like going in on a group gift or joining a co-op—with people you'll never meet. Mutual funds allow a group of investors to combine their cash and invest it. By pooling their money together, mutual fund investors can sample a broader range of stocks or bonds than they could if they were trying to buy the stocks and bonds on their own.

The Mechanics

Many people think of mutual funds as "products." But when you buy a mutual fund, you're actually buying an ownership stake in a corporation that in turn hires a money manager to invest its money. The price of a single ownership stake in a fund is called its net asset value, or NAV. Invest $1,000 in a fund with an NAV of $118.74, for example, and you will get 8.42 shares. ($1,000÷$118.74=8.42.)

The fund manager combines your money with that of other investors. Taken altogether, those investments are called the fund's assets. The fund manager invests the fund's assets, typically by buying stocks, bonds, or a combination of the two. (Some funds buy more complicated security types.) These stocks or bonds are often referred to as a fund's "holdings," and all of a fund's holdings together are its "portfolio." A fund's type depends on the kinds of securities it holds. For example, a stock fund invests in stocks, while a small-company stock fund focuses on the stocks of small companies.

What you get as an investor or shareholder is a portion of that portfolio. Regardless of how much or how little you invest, your shares are the portfolio in miniature.

For example, Vanguard 500 Index's three largest holdings are General Electric (3.0% of its portfolio on Dec. 31, 2003), Microsoft (2.88%), and ExxonMobil (2.62%). A $1,000 investment in that fund means that you own about $30 of General Electric, $28.80 of Microsoft, and $26.20 of ExxonMobil. In fact, you own all 500 stocks in the fund's portfolio.

A piece of the pie	It is possible to own a fraction of a mutual fund share. For instance, if a fund's share price is $60 and you have $2,500 to invest, you can purchase 41.67 shares. This makes mutual funds a more flexible investment than stocks.

Mutual funds offer some notable benefits to investors.

1. They don't demand large up-front investments.

If you had just $1,000 to invest, it would be difficult for you to assemble a varied basket of stocks or bonds on your own. For example, with $1,000, you could buy one share of stock from the largest U.S. company, then one from the next largest, and so on, but it's likely that you'd run out of money sometime before purchasing your 20th stock.

If you bought a mutual fund, though, you would be able to sample many more types of stocks or bonds with that same $1,000. You can make an initial investment in several funds with just $1,000 in hand; $2,500 will get you into many more funds. If you invest through an Individual Retirement Account, you can often get your foot in the door with even less than $1,000. You can even buy some funds for as little as $50 per month if you agree to invest a certain dollar amount each month. (We'll cover different investment methods in an upcoming lesson.)

2. They're easy to buy and sell.

Whether you're buying funds on your own or hiring a broker or financial planner to do it for you, funds are easy to buy. Once a fund company has your money, it often takes just a phone call or mouse click to buy shares in a fund. Of course, there are exceptions: Closed funds, for example, no longer accept money from new shareholders.

You don't have to be a tycoon to invest in mutual funds. Many funds will accept initial investments of as little as $1,000—even less if you commit to making investments on a monthly basis. And just think: For only $1,000, you'll get a stake in every single security that the mutual fund owns!

Something for the little guy

By the same token, it's also easy to sell a fund. Unlike many other security types, such as individual stocks, you don't need to find a buyer when it's time to unload your shares. Instead, the vast majority of mutual funds offer daily redemptions, meaning that the fund company will give you cash whenever you're ready to sell. Investors who own closed funds can also sell at any time.

3. They're regulated.

Mutual fund managers can't take your money and head for some remote island somewhere. Security exists through regulations set by the Investment Company Act of 1940. After the stock-market madness of the two decades prior to 1940, which revealed some big investors' tendencies to take advantage of small investors (to put it nicely), the government stepped in to put safeguards in place for investors.

Thanks to the Investment Company Act of 1940 (often called "the '40 Act"), your mutual fund is a regulated investment company (regulated by the Securities & Exchange Commission) and you, as a mutual fund investor, are an owner of that company. As with other types of companies, mutual funds have boards of directors that represent the fund's shareholders. Among other duties, the board is charged with ensuring that the best available managers are running the fund and that shareholders aren't overpaying for the managers' services. For example, the board of directors at Fidelity Magellan has hired Fidelity to run the fund on behalf of shareholders.

The fact that mutual funds are regulated shouldn't give investors a false sense of security, however. Mutual funds are not insured or guaranteed. You can lose money in a mutual fund because a fund's value is based on the value of all of its portfolio holdings. If the holdings lose value, so will the fund. The odds that you will lose all of your money in a mutual fund are very slim, though—all of the stocks or bonds in the portfolio would have to go belly up for that to happen. And history suggests that such a mass implosion is unlikely in the vast majority of fund types.

4. They're professionally managed.

If you plan to buy individual stocks and bonds, you need to know how to read a company's cash-flow statement or assess the likelihood that a given company will fail to meet its debt obligations. Such in-depth financial knowledge is not required to invest in a mutual fund, however. While mutual fund investors should have a basic understanding of how the stock and bond markets work, you pay your fund managers to select individual securities for you.

Still, mutual funds are not fairy-tale investments. As you will learn in later sessions, some funds are expensive and others perform poorly. But overall, mutual funds are good investments for those who don't have the money, time, or interest necessary to compile a collection of securities on their own.

Fearless Facts

▶ Mutual funds allow people to combine their cash and invest it.

▶ When you buy a mutual fund, you're buying shares in a corporation. That corporation, in turn, hires a money manager to select investments for it.

▶ Mutual funds typically invest in stocks, bonds, or a combination of the two; taken together, those stocks and/or bonds are called the portfolio.

▶ Your share of the portfolio is essentially the entire portfolio in miniature. Mutual funds don't demand large up-front investments. Thus, you can build a diversified portfolio without having to pony up boatloads of cash to purchase individual stocks and bonds.

▶ You can also easily buy and sell mutual funds, either on your own or through a third party, such as a broker.

▶ Funds are regulated to ensure that your fund's manager won't take your money and run.

▶ Like other types of corporations, each mutual fund has a board of directors that's charged with safeguarding shareholders' interests. For example, fund boards help oversee the investment manager and determine whether the manager's fees are appropriate.

▶ Funds also enable you to leave the rigorous task of security analysis and portfolio management to the professional money managers running the fund.

Quiz

1   Investing in a stock mutual fund does not offer you:

    a   Ownership of a corporation.

    b   Regulation by the SEC.

    c   An insured investment.

Answers to this quiz can be found on page 203

2   A fund's price per share is called its:

    a   Stock price.

    b   NAV (net asset value).

    c   Initial investment.

3   Who owns Fidelity Magellan Fund?

    a   Fidelity.

    b   Fidelity Magellan's board of directors.

    c   Fidelity Magellan's shareholders.

4   Mutual funds are:

    a   Insured.

    b   Regulated.

    c   Guaranteed.

5   Which of the following statements is false?

    a   When you own a fund, you own a piece of all the securities in that fund.

    b   When you sell the fund, the fund transfers ownership of those securities to you.

    c   You can sell a closed fund, but you can't buy one.

11

Worksheet

What do your shares in a mutual fund represent?

Look at your past mutual fund or 401(k) statements.
Were there periods in which your fund lost money? ◯ yes ◯ no
What were the factors that might have contributed to those losses?

What are some advantages of investing in mutual funds rather than in individual stocks and bonds?

Why is the ability to buy a fraction of a mutual fund share so important?
How does it help you as an individual investor?

Mutual funds are often considered "safe" compared with individual stocks. Has your experience with funds and individual stocks shown this to be true? In what way?

Lesson 102: Mutual Funds and NAVs

In the previous lesson, we examined the mutual fund's NAV, its net asset value (or price per share). NAVs seem similar to stock prices; after all, both represent the price of one share of an investment. Both appear in newspapers and on financial Web sites. But that's where the similarities between NAVs and stock prices end.

Calculating the NAV

A mutual fund calculates its NAV by adding up the current value of all the stocks, bonds, and other securities (including cash) in its portfolio, subtracting the manager's salary and other operating expenses, and then dividing that figure by the fund's total number of shares. For example, a fund with 500,000 shares that owns $9 million in stocks and $1 million in cash has an NAV of $20.

$$\frac{\$9 \text{ million in stocks} \oplus \$1 \text{ million in cash}}{500,000 \text{ shares}} \ominus \$20 \text{ NAV}$$

So Alike But So Very Different

NAVs and stock prices differ in five important ways.

Difference One. Stock prices change throughout the trading day, but mutual fund NAVs are calculated only once each day, based on the value of their stocks or bonds at the time the market closes. When you purchase a mutual fund, you buy shares at the NAV as of that day's close. As a result, you don't necessarily know the exact NAV of the fund at the time you put in your order to buy or sell. If you place an order early in a given day, you're likely to get that day's closing price for the fund. If you make your order later in the day or after trading has ended, you'll get the following day's closing price.

NAVs need not apply	There's one kind of mutual fund investor who never has to worry about NAVs. Money market funds, which many investors use for short-term goals, have NAVs that are fixed. That means that there are no tax implications when you sell your shares, though you do have to pay taxes on any income from a money market fund you hold in your taxable account.

Difference Two. Stock investors typically specify how many shares they'd like to buy, and buy shares of a given stock in even lots, such as 50 shares of Coca-Cola or 100 shares of Microsoft. By contrast, most fund investors purchase funds in dollar amounts rather than share amounts. As we noted in Lesson 101, fund companies willingly issue fractional shares. For example, if you have $1,250 that you'd like to put into a fund with an NAV of $14, you'll get exactly 89.286 shares.

Difference Three. Stocks have a fixed number of shares available. To change its number of shares, a company can either issue new shares or buy back its own shares in the market. By contrast, mutual funds generally have an unlimited number of shares, and the number changes on a daily basis, depending on how many shares investors buy and sell that day.

Difference Four. You can determine whether a stock is a bargain or not by its current price relative to a "fair value" price, based on such information as earnings estimates or cash flows. (This process is known as "valuing" a stock.) With mutual funds, however, NAV is tied to the current value of the fund's underlying holdings. Calculating a fair price for an entire mutual fund's portfolio, while theoretically possible, would be a cumbersome process, particularly when you consider that many funds hold well more than 100 stocks or bonds.

Difference Five. You can often use changes in a stock's price to gauge how well a stock is performing. Mutual funds, however, distribute any income or capital gains they realize to shareholders as dividends, which, in turn, causes their NAVs to fluctuate. Unless you account for such distributions, you could be underestimating a fund's actual performance by looking solely at its NAV. To accurately gauge a fund's performance, you need to examine its total return, which takes into account both the appreciation of the fund's holdings as well as any distributions the fund has paid out. (We'll explore this topic in our next lesson.)

Uses of NAV

After learning a bit more about NAVs, you may be thinking, "What the heck *can* I use NAV for?" Well, NAVs do provide you with some idea of what your investment is worth each day. And because funds calculate daily NAVs, investors can buy and sell each day. Daily access to NAVs also reassures you that your investment is being watched over, valued, and reported on.

The incredible shrinking NAV	Many investors seek out high-yielding bond funds: Wouldn't we all rather live off the income from our portfolios than tap into our savings? Investors should be aware, however, that some of the highest-yielding funds are actually just returning your own principal to you. That's right—part of their yield is your own money. If a fund shows a steady decline in its NAV over a period of many years, that could be an indication that your manager is robbing Peter (you) to pay Paul (also you).

Fearless Facts

▶ Your fund is required to publish its NAV at the end of each trading day. The mutual fund shop calculates its NAV by combining the current value of all its assets, subtracting the expenses incurred in the running of the fund, and dividing that figure by the number of the fund's outstanding shares.

▶ Stock prices change all day long as investors buy and sell portions of the company. NAVs are calculated just once per day.

▶ Everyone's welcome at a mutual fund. Funds generally have an unlimited number of shares available (unless they're closed funds—something we'll explore later). Companies, on the other hand, generally have a fixed number of shares available.

▶ NAV can't tell you much about the progress, success, or popularity of a mutual fund. Stock prices, on the other hand, can give you a clue as to the company's success or failure in the marketplace.

Quiz

1   A fund with $10 million in stock holdings and $2 million in cash
(after expenses are taken into account), and 1 million shares outstanding
has an NAV of:

Answers to this
quiz can be found
on page 203

    a $8.30.

    b $1.

    c $12.

2   You buy a fund at 11:00 (Eastern Standard Time) on Tuesday morning.
In most cases, what NAV do you get?

    a   The NAV at Monday's close.

    b   The NAV at 11:00 a.m. EST on Tuesday.

    c   The NAV at Tuesday's close.

3   A fund's number of shares outstanding increases from 1 million to
2 million in a year. Over the course of that year, what happens to the
fund's NAV?

    a   It depends on how its underlying portfolio holdings perform.

    b   It expands.

    c   It contracts.

4   Fund A's NAV is $10 while Fund B's is $110, and both funds have
minimum initial investments of $100. Which fund is within reach of
someone with just $100 to invest?

    a   Fund A.

    b   Fund B.

    c   Both funds.

Worksheet

If you are trying to decide between two funds that have identical portfolios and identical asset bases—and even have the same manager—why might their NAVs be different? Is one a better "bargain" than the other? How can you tell?

A fund holds $600,000 worth of stocks and $200,000 in cash after accounting for management fees and expenses. It has 50,000 shares outstanding, held by 15,000 investors. What's your estimate of its NAV?

List some of the ways in which NAV is different from a stock price.

Does looking at your mutual fund's NAV tell you how that fund has performed over time? Why or why not?

Lesson 103: Understanding Total Return

There's a relationship between net asset value (NAV), yield, and total return, but it's complicated. Did you know that a fund's NAV can fall and you can still make money? Or that a fund can yield less than 1%—in fact, it can yield nothing at all—and yet its returns can still be at the top of the charts?

Before we go further, though, let's review the two key components of total return. You can earn money from your investment in two ways: income (often called yield) and capital appreciation.

Income

A fund's income payout, or yield, tends to interest those investors who need regular income because they don't necessarily have to tap into their principal for their day-to-day living expenses. Savings accounts and CDs pay income, but so do most bonds and some stocks. If you own a mutual fund that buys income-paying stocks or bonds, the manager passes on any income to shareholders (after taking expenses off the top, of course).

If you're primarily interested in higher-yielding funds, the first thing to look for is a fund with a low expense ratio—preferably one that charges 1% per year or less. Focusing on funds with lower expenses can boost your yield because expenses are always subtracted from any income a fund might receive from its holdings.

Cheap out

Yield can be calculated in a variety of ways. Morningstar calculates yield for the past 12 months. In other words, we add up all of a fund's income payments over the past year and divide the total by the most recent month-end NAV.

Capital Appreciation

The second key way you can gain from a fund is through capital appreciation—that is, if one or more of your fund's holdings is selling for a higher price than it was when the manager purchased it. If the manager sells the new, pricier stock or bond, the fund clocks what is called a capital gain. And even if the manager simply hangs on to the stock or bond that has gained in value, the fund will enjoy capital appreciation; in other words, its NAV will increase. That's because the NAV is a reflection of the value of all of the securities in a fund at a given point in time.

Distributions

As counterintuitive as it may seem, looking at a fund's NAV in isolation isn't always the best way to check up on its performance. That's because the NAV is vulnerable to changes that don't necessarily affect the true value of the fund.

For example, a fund's NAV will change whenever a fund makes a payment to its shareholders, otherwise known as a distribution. By law, mutual funds must distribute any income they have received from their stocks or bonds, as well as any capital gains they have realized from their holdings. (A fund "realizes" a capital gain when it sells a stock or bond for a higher price than when it was purchased.) But whenever a fund passes along either income or capital gains to shareholders, its NAV drops. If a fund with an NAV of $10 makes a $4 distribution, its NAV slips to $6.

Despite the shrunken NAV, shareholders are none the poorer. They still have $10: $6 in the fund and another $4 in cash. Unless they need the $4 in income to spend, most investors will reinvest their distributions back into the fund; in other words, they instruct the fund company to use that cash to buy new shares of the fund. Most total-return numbers reported in newspapers or on the Web, including those used by Morningstar, assume that you reinvest your distributions.

Don't confuse annualized returns with total returns. Annualized returns are average annual compound returns. They tell you what a fund earned, on average, over a period of time—say, 10 years. Total return, on the other hand, is more specific; a fund's total return is its complete gain or loss over a particular time period.

It's all good

Back to Total Return

Total return encompasses everything we have discussed thus far: changes in NAV caused by appreciation or depreciation of the underlying portfolio, payment of any income (yield) or capital-gains distributions, and reinvestment of those distributions.

Here's how it works. Say you buy 10 shares of Fund A at $9 per share. After a few months, the fund's NAV rises to $12. The fund sells some of its winning stocks and makes a $2 per-share capital-gains distribution. It makes no income distributions. As a result, the fund's NAV falls to $10. Your distribution of $20 ($2 x 10 shares) is used to buy two more shares at the new $10 price. Finally, say the fund's NAV rises again, this time to $11 share.

So what is the yield on this investment? Zero, because it has not paid out any income. What about your overall return? Well, if you used only your NAV to calculate return, your shares would be worth the fund's final $11 NAV times your initial 10 shares, or $110. That's an NAV return of 22% on your original investment.

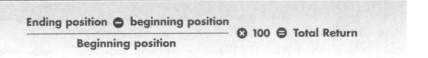

But that figure would be inaccurate because you need to factor in the capital-gains distribution that you reinvested. Add that back in and you'll find your investment is actually worth that $110 plus the $22 your two new shares are worth, for a grand total of $132. Your total return is really 47%. Not too shabby.

Remember that there are trade-offs. If you're trying to get more yield, you could wind up losing ground in the long run. Here's why: When you pocket a fund's income rather than reinvesting it back into your fund, you shrink your principal (the money that is in the fund, working for you). That means that you're cutting off some potential and allowing yourself to spend NOW rather than save for later.

Examine the trade-offs

Fearless Facts

▶ The most important measurement of your fund's performance is its total return (not its NAV or its yield).

▶ Total return includes changes in NAV caused by appreciation or depreciation in the underlying portfolio, payment of any income (yield) or capital-gains distributions, and reinvestment of those distributions.

▶ Remember: A declining NAV doesn't mean that your fund's value is declining. A fund often makes distributions to shareholders, which are subtracted from its NAV. You still get the money, but in a different form.

▶ A fund's yield is income that the fund distributes to you, the investor. Yield has more to do with the kinds of assets in the fund's portfolio (bonds and dividend-paying stocks) than with the quality of the fund itself.

Quiz

1   Total return takes into account:

> **a**   The change in a fund's NAV.
>
> **b**   Income distributions.
>
> **c**   The change in a fund's NAV and the reinvested distributions (such as yield and capital gains) the fund makes during that time.

Answers to this quiz can be found on page 204

2   When mutual funds pass along distributions to shareholders, their NAVs:

> **a**   Rise.
>
> **b**   Fall.
>
> **c**   Stay the same.

3   What does yield represent?

> **a**   A fund's income distributions over the past 12 months.
>
> **b**   A fund's capital-gains distributions over the past 12 months.
>
> **c**   A fund's total return.

4   What is reinvestment?

> **a**   Taking income or capital-gains distributions in cash.
>
> **b**   Automatically putting income or capital-gains distributions back into the fund.
>
> **c**   Adding to your position in a fund.

5   You bought 10 shares of a fund with an NAV of $10. It makes a $5 per share distribution, and its NAV falls to $5. If you reinvest, you have:

> **a**   Lost $50.
>
> **b**   Ten shares of the fund.
>
> **c**   Twenty shares of the fund.

Worksheet

When you make investment decisions, are you trying to generate income, capital gains, or both? What is the difference?

Consider the following investment decisions:

In January, you buy 100 shares of the American Heritage Fund for $5 per share. The fund's NAV increases to $9 in June. Your manager trims some stocks and passes on a $3-per-share distribution to you. What's the new NAV?

You decide to use your distribution ($3 x 100 shares) to reinvest. How many new shares can you buy at the new NAV?

What is the overall return on the fund? (Hint: First, calculate the effect of the new NAV on your original shares and compare it with your original $100 investment.)

continued...

If possible, examine your own funds and answer the following questions:

At what points in the coming year are your funds scheduled to make capital-gains distributions?

How many funds in your portfolio offer a yield? Are you reinvesting that money?

Are you reinvesting any capital gains that your funds are paying out?

Make the Fine Print
Work for You

Lesson 104: Fund Costs

These days, every time you purchase something, you get a detailed receipt. With a receipt, you know exactly where your money is going and just how smart—or ridiculous—your spending decisions have been.

Not so with mutual funds. As a mutual fund investor, you'll never write a check to a mutual fund for its services. That means you'll never know exactly where your money is going unless you're very, very vigilant. Any service charges for mutual funds come right off the top of your investment or straight out of your returns. Because costs are deducted this way, many investors aren't even aware of how much they're paying for their mutual funds.

Mutual fund fees can be broken down into two main categories: one-time fees and ongoing annual expenses. Not all funds charge one-time fees, but all funds charge ongoing annual fees of some sort. Return figures that you see for mutual funds in newspapers, annual reports, and financial Web sites typically don't reflect one-time fees, but ongoing expenses are almost always deducted from return figures that you see in public sources.

One-Time Fees

There are three types of one-time fees that you may pay, all of which are usually charged when you buy or sell a fund. Remember, not all funds charge these fees; to find out if a particular fund does, consult its prospectus or its Web site or call the fund's toll-free number.

1. Sales Commissions

Commissions are commonly called loads. If you have to pay a sales charge, or commission, when you purchase shares in the fund, that's known as a front-end load; a sales charge when you sell is a back-end load. (Some back-end loads phase out if you hold the fund for a certain number of years.) You might also pay a level load, or a percentage of your return each year for a series of five or so years.

Share and share alike?	In the past 10 years, fund companies have introduced different share classes, primarily because they know that it's an easy way to shift around their cost structures. These share classes all represent exactly the same thing— exposure to some portfolio of stocks and bonds—but their fees are organized differently. Here are some general rules of thumb:
Class A shares:	Often come with front-end loads and carry 12b-1 fees.
Class B shares:	Usually have a back-end load of some kind as well as an ongoing 12b-1 fee to cover marketing and distribution costs.
Class C shares:	Sometimes these shares don't have loads at all, but fund companies push their 12b-1 fees way up. High ongoing fees mean that the annual return data of C shares can look pretty grim relative to the other share classes'.

Loads come directly out of your investment, effectively reducing the amount of money that you're putting to work. For example, if you made a $10,000 investment in a fund that carried a 4.5% front-end load, only $9,550 would be invested in the fund. The remaining $450 would go to the advisor or broker who sold you the fund.

Basically, loads are payment to the advisor who sells you the invest-ment; it's his or her compensation for doling out financial advice. So if you're buying a load fund, be sure you're getting solid investment advice in return.

Front-end charges can't be more than 8.5%, and they're generally no higher than about 6%. Back-end loads often start at about 5% or 6%, and many funds reduce them each year that you leave your money in the fund. You might find that when you buy a fund, the exit fee is 5%. If you wait to sell it for four years, the fee could fall by a few per-centage points. If this is the case with your fund, your broker will probably call it a contingent deferred sales fee or something like that.

2. Redemption Fees

Redemption fees differ from loads in that they are usually paid direct-ly to the fund—in other words, they go back into the pot rather than to the broker or advisor. You may have to pay a redemption fee if you hold a fund for only a short period of time. In most cases, this time frame is less than 90 days, but it can be as long as a few years.

These fees are an attempt to discourage short-term traders from mov-ing in and out of a fund. The fees are put in place for the protection of the shareholders and the fund managers. Why are these short-term traders (often called market-timers) bad for everyone else? Market-timers may attempt to cash out of their investments all at once. A rash of sales can force fund managers to sell securities that they don't really want to sell; after all, they have to get the cash from somewhere to meet the redemption calls. And if management has to sell securities that have gained in value, it may also pass along a taxable capital-gains distribution to shareholders who remain behind. So in a sense, redemption fees are the friend of long-term investors because they'll never have to pay them, and the fees (in theory, at least) keep timers at arm's length.

3. Account-Maintenance Fees

Some fund companies charge account-maintenance fees, but such fees are usually for smaller accounts. Some Vanguard funds, for example, charge shareholders a $10 account-maintenance fee if their account balances dip below $10,000. Shareholders pay this fee each year until their account values rise above $10,000.

Big bargains

When a mutual fund's assets balloon, the fund shop will often pass along savings to shareholders in the form of lower annual expenses. A fund with a 1% expense ratio and $20 million in assets receives $200,000 per year to pay the fund's manager and cover administrative costs—certainly not a paltry sum, but not anything for Donald Trump to write home about.

But say the fund's manager makes savvy choices and the fund suddenly gets a lot of attention. If assets grow to $1 billion, that same fund collects a princely $10 million each year. The fund could pocket that extra cash and call it a very profitable day, but lots of funds behave more charitably toward their shareholders by paring down annual fees.

Ongoing Expenses

While the fees we've discussed so far are levied by only certain types of funds, all funds annually charge—and deduct from your return— the following fees.

1. Expense Ratio

Most fund costs are bundled into the expense ratio, which is listed in a fund's prospectus and annual report as a percentage of assets. For example, if ABC Fund has assets of $200 million and charges $2 million in expenses, it will report an expense ratio of 1%.

The expense ratio has several parts. The largest element is usually the management fee, which goes to the fund family overseeing the portfolio. There are also administrative fees, which pay for things such as mailing out all those prospectuses, annual reports, and account statements. These fees are periodically deducted from the fund's overall assets. These deductions reduce the fund's portfolio value.

The 12b-1 fee can be another large component of the expense ratio; such fees are levied by roughly half of all funds. These fees are named after an SEC rule that allows fund companies to use portfolio assets to cover a fund's distribution and advertising costs. These expenses can be as high as 1% of assets. Fees that fund families pay to no-transaction-fee networks, which we'll learn about in a later lesson, often get charged to fund shareholders via 12b-1 fees.

2. Brokerage Costs

These costs are incurred by a fund as it buys and sells securities, in much the same way you might pay brokerage fees if you were trading stocks online. These costs are not included in the expense ratio, but instead are listed separately in a fund's annual report or statement of additional information.

This figure excludes some hard-to-pin-down expenses. For example, when a fund invests in over-the-counter stocks (typically stocks traded on the Nasdaq exchange), it doesn't pay the broker a set fee. Rather, the cost of the transaction is built into the stock price. It is a trading expense that comes out of your return, but fund companies don't report it separately.

3. Interest Expense

If a fund borrows money to buy securities—not a very common practice among mutual funds—it incurs interest costs. This is particularly common in mutual funds that engage in long/short strategies. Such expenses are also taken out of the shareholders' annual return.

What's Reasonable?

As you can see, mutual funds are far from a free lunch. But you can keep more of what you earn by sticking with low-cost funds. What qualifies as low cost? That depends on how long you plan to own an investment, and what type of fund you're talking about.

When it comes to bond funds, no-load offerings with the lowest possible expense ratios are best for most investors. That's because the difference between the best- and worst-performing bond fund is pretty slim; bond-fund returns differ by just small amounts, so every dollar that goes to expenses really hurts your return. Our advice: Avoid bond funds with expense ratios above 0.75%.

On the stock side, a load fund may make a perfectly fine investment, if you're a long-term investor. But load-fund investors should look for funds with fairly low annual costs, such as those sponsored by American Funds. Their total costs (including sales fees) over a period of years are actually more moderate than those of many no-load funds.

Pinching Pennies Adds Up

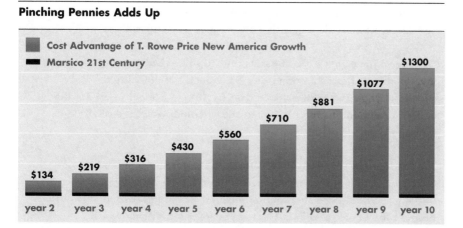

T. Rowe Price New America Growth charges 0.98% while Marsico 21st Century charges 1.55%. That small difference can add up in a big way over time. Say you invest $10,000 in each for 10 years. If both funds produce a 10% annualized return on their portfolios, the difference after expenses is more than $1,000. Because the money saved in each year compounds at a higher rate in the cheaper fund, that small initial advantage adds up to more than 10% of your initial investment.

You can find plenty of good funds investing in large-company stocks that charge less than 1% per year in expenses. As with bond funds, the range of returns doesn't vary much, so lower expenses give a fund a decided edge on the competition.

With small-company and foreign-stock funds, expect to pay closer to 1.5% annually. Fund companies contend that it takes portfolio managers and their research teams more effort—and more money—to research tiny companies and foreign firms because there isn't as much readily available information about them. Not surprisingly, these funds pass a portion of their extra costs on to you, their shareholders.

Bleak math	It seems strange that tiny little fees would make a big difference in fund performance, right? By using some simple math, you'll see why low-cost funds often outdo expensive offerings in the long run.
	Consider a fund with $100 in assets and 10 shares outstanding. The fund invests in local firms that don't pay a dividend but do enjoy a successful year. The portfolio increases by 10%—a banner year! But the expense ratio on this fund is 1%, so shareholders won't see all of that nice gain.
	The fund's initial NAV is $100/10 shares = $10 per share. If we had no expenses to contend with, fund assets would grow by $10 ($110) and the NAV that each shareholder enjoyed would increase to $11. But because the expense ratio is 1%, the portfolio is suddenly worth just $108.90. That means that an investor's take-home return is 8.90%, not 10%.

At Morningstar, we put a good deal of emphasis on mutual fund costs, not only because they're often hidden, but because we think favoring lower-cost funds is an easy way to improve your long-term results. We've found that over long time periods, lower-cost funds tend to outperform higher-cost funds. And costs are the only thing about a fund that are absolutely predictable, year in and year out.

Fearless Facts

▶ The hard truth is that you're going to have to pay fund companies to manage your money. Mutual fund companies quote these charges as a percentage of total assets. Remember that you pay this percentage every year.

▶ You can find this figure, called the expense ratio, in the prospectus. Fund shops are required to disclose it.

▶ If you're a do-it-yourself investor, it's best to stick with low-cost funds and stay away from offerings that carry loads, or sales charges. History suggests that cheaper vehicles perform better than more expensive ones over the long haul.

▶ Brokers and advisors may steer you toward load funds because such offerings have a commission structure. But be vigilant: Compare your fund with other, lower-cost portfolios to assess whether differences in quality are real or imagined. And if you do opt for a load fund, be sure that you're taking full advantage of the professional advice that is supposed to come hand-in-hand with it. After all, you're paying for it!

▶ Not all no-load fund companies are strictly that, so be sure you know exactly what you're getting. Fidelity, for example, is a shop known for no-load offerings, but it has several funds that come with sales charges for certain kinds of accounts.

Quiz

1 All fund investors pay:

a   Redemption fees.

b   Annual expenses.

c   Account-maintenance fees.

Answers to this quiz can be found on page 204

2 When do you pay a fund's load?

a   When you buy the fund.

b   When you sell the fund.

c   It depends on the load structure.

3 What does the expense ratio include?

a   12b-1 fees.

b   Brokerage fees.

c   Interest expense.

4 Why should you favor low-cost funds?

a   Because the less money you pay in expenses, the more money that goes to you.

b   Because low-cost funds tend to perform better than high-cost funds.

c   Both.

5 A 1.5% expense ratio is acceptable for which type of fund?

a   A foreign-stock fund.

b   A U.S. fund investing in large companies.

c   A bond fund.

Worksheet

Look at a fund you own or a mutual fund you're considering as an investment. What costs are associated with it? Are there sales loads? Distribution fees? Do these fees decrease over time?

Why are low-cost mutual funds a better choice than funds with higher expenses?

Examine one of your mutual fund holdings. What was this fund's return over the past year? What percentage return would you have if the fund did not charge expenses?

Do you own any bond funds? If so, how do expenses affect how your fund stacks up relative to other bond funds? Do those expenses seem more or less important than the expenses of your stock funds?

Lesson 105: Mutual Funds and Taxes

Thus far, we have lauded mutual funds' virtues. They don't require a large up-front investment. They're professionally managed. They're easy to buy and sell. And if you shop carefully, you can limit how much you have to pay to own them.

But there is one thing that mutual funds may not be: tax-friendly. In the following section, we'll explore reasons for this weakness and examine the ways in which you can minimize its impact on your bottom line.

Funds, Capital Gains, and Income

As we've already noted, mutual funds must pass along to their shareholders any realized capital gains that are not offset by realized losses by the end of their accounting year. Mutual fund managers "realize" a capital gain whenever they sell a security for more money than they paid for it. Conversely, they realize a loss when they sell a security for less than the purchase price. If gains outweigh losses, the managers must distribute the difference to fund shareholders.

Fund managers must also distribute any income that their securities generate. Bond funds typically pay out yields, but so do some stock funds if the stocks they own pay dividends.

As you may recall, when paying out capital gains or income, funds multiply the number of shares you own by the per-share distribution amount. You'll receive a check in the mail for the total amount of the distribution. Or, if you choose to reinvest all distributions, the fund will instead use the money to buy more shares of the fund for you. After the distribution is made, the fund's NAV will drop by the same amount as the distribution. Fund companies often make capital-gains distributions in December, but they can happen anytime during the year.

Another difference...

When you own an individual stock or bond, you pay income tax each year on any dividends or interest you receive. But you won't have to pay any capital-gains taxes until you actually sell the stock (and even then you'll only have to pay if you've made a profit in that stock or bond). Not so with mutual funds. As a fund shareholder, you will owe income tax on any dividends in the year you receive or reinvest them. And in addition to paying taxes on the personal capital gains that you may shoulder when you sell your shares, you will also pay taxes each year on any capital gains the fund has paid out, even if you haven't sold one of your own shares. That's because the law requires mutual funds to distribute capital gains to shareholders if the manager sells securities for a profit and doesn't offset it with a loss.

Distributions and Taxes

Unless you own your mutual fund through a 401(k) plan, an IRA, or some other type of tax-deferred account, you'll owe taxes on that distribution—even if you reinvested it (used the distribution to buy more shares of the fund). That is particularly painful if you have just purchased the fund because you are paying taxes for gains you didn't get.

Let's use an example to illustrate. Suppose you invest $250 in Fund D on Monday. The fund's NAV is $25, so you are able to buy 10 shares. If the fund makes a $5-per-share distribution on Tuesday (which means you have been handed a $50 distribution), and you reinvest, your investment is still worth the same $250:

> **Monday 10.0 shares @ $25 ⊖ $250**
> **Tuesday 12.5 shares @ $20 ⊖ $250**

The trouble is, you now owe capital-gains taxes on that $50 distribution. The current long-term capital-gains tax rate is 15% for anyone in the 25% or higher bracket and 5% for those in 10% to 15% brackets. If you're in the higher tax bracket, you'd have to pay $7.50 in taxes on that long-term capital gain. (Shorter-term capital gains are taxed at a higher rate.)

If you immediately sold the fund, the whole thing would be a wash, as the capital gains would be offset by a capital loss. The distribution lowers the NAV, so the amount of taxes you would pay would be lower than if you sold the fund years from now. Still, most investors would rather pay taxes later than sooner. And we're guessing that if you just invested in the fund, you weren't planning to turn around and sell it right away.

Funds occasionally can add insult to injury by paying out a large capital-gains distribution in a year in which the fund lost money. In
other words, you can lose money in a fund and still have to pay taxes.
In 2000, for example, many technology funds made big capital-gains
distributions, even though almost all of them were in the red for the
year. Although the funds lost money during the year, they sold some
stocks bought at lower prices and had to pay out capital-gains as a
result. Technology-fund investors lost money to both the market and
Uncle Sam that year.

Indecent exposure   In order to discover the potential capital-gains exposure you're facing,
you'll need to dig deep into the fund literature or consult an outside
source. Check the fund's distribution schedule, which is often in its prospectus, to figure out when the next payment could be coming your way.
Toward the end of the year, many fund companies also publish estimates
of the capital gains they may distribute later on in the year.

Avoiding Overtaxation

Alleviate tax headaches by following these tips:

Tip One. Ask a fund company if a distribution is imminent before buying a fund, especially if you are investing late in the calendar year.
(Funds often make capital-gains distributions in December.) Find out
if the fund has tax-loss carryforwards—that is, if it has booked capital
losses in previous years that can be used to offset capital gains in future
years. That means the fund could be tax-friendly in the future.

Tip Two. Place tax-inefficient funds in tax-deferred accounts, such as IRAS or 401(k)s. If a fund has a turnover rate of 100% or more, it's a good indication that limiting the tax collector's cut isn't one of the manager's objectives.

Tip Three. Search for extremely low-turnover funds—in other words, funds in which the manager isn't doing a lot of buying and selling and therefore isn't realizing a lot of taxable capital gains. A fund with a turnover rate of 50% isn't four times more tax-efficient than a fund with a 200% turnover rate. But funds with turnover ratios below 10% tend to be tax-efficient. You can find turnover rates on Morningstar, as well as in your fund's annual report.

Tip Four. Favor funds run by managers who have their own wealth invested in their funds, such as Third Avenue Value's Marty Whitman or the managers of Tweedy, Browne Global Value. These managers are likely to be tax conscious because at least some of the money they have invested in their funds is in taxable accounts.

The SEC will soon require fund families to disclose whether their managers have a stake in the funds they manage, and if so, how much. In the meantime, however, Morningstar is surveying fund managers for this information and making it available to Premium Members of Morningstar.com.

Tip Five. If you want to buy a bond fund and are in a higher tax bracket, consider municipal-bond funds. Income from these funds is usually tax-exempt.

Low turnover: No panacea	Tax-conscious investors often pay attention to a fund's turnover rate because funds with very low turnover (less than 10%) tend to be relatively tax-efficient. But investors should be aware that if the manager of such a fund leaves, the new manager could sell his or her predecessor's long-held stocks. If the fund has scored big gains from some of those holdings, fund shareholders could be vulnerable to a big tax bill when the new manager sells.

Tip Six. Consider tax-managed funds. These funds use a series of strategies to limit their taxable distributions. Vanguard, Fidelity, and T. Rowe Price all offer tax-managed funds.

Tip Seven. Although you can't control the timing of your fund's taxable distributions, you can time your own fund purchases and sales with an eye toward keeping a lid on how much you pay in taxes. For example, if you expect a fund you own to make a big capital-gains distribution in a given year, you might consider selling a fund that you've lost money on (particularly if it has been a poor performer relative to other funds with a similar investment approach). That way, you can offset one fund's gain with a loss from the losing fund.

Even following these tips, it can be difficult to find a fund that's consistently tax-efficient. But don't get so caught up in tax considerations that you overlook good performance. After all, a tax-efficient fund that returns 7% after taxes is no match for a tax-inefficient fund that nets 15% after Uncle Sam takes his share. (You can find after-tax returns in our Fund Reports on Morningstar.com.) In the end, it is what you keep, not what you give away, that counts.

Fearless Facts

▶ Remember that taxes can be a mutual fund's Achilles' heel. Investors have no control over when their funds realize taxable capital gains and make taxable distributions. That means that fund managers can buy and sell stocks or bonds no matter what the tax implications are.

▶ Avoid tax burdens by holding funds in a tax-deferred account—an IRA or a 401(k).

▶ Consider tax-managed funds, fielded by some of the biggest mutual fund shops, such as Vanguard, Fidelity, and T. Rowe Price. Such funds are explicitly managed to limit Uncle Sam's cut of your return.

▶ Find out if the fund plans to make a capital-gains distribution before you buy. Alternatively, avoid buying funds toward the end of each calendar year; Morningstar has found that funds usually make their distributions in the last quarter of the year.

▶ Seek funds with very low turnover rates. Turnover rates reflect the pace of the manager's trading activity. Funds with low turnover rates tend to be more tax-efficient than funds with high turnover rates.

▶ Favor funds that favor shareholders. A great way to find such offerings is to identify mutual funds that require the managers to invest. They're likely to be pretty tax-conscious because they'll be hit by whatever tax burdens face the fund's shareholders.

Quiz

1   Who controls how much funds distribute in taxable gains and income each year?

- **a**   You, the fund shareholder.
- **b**   The fund manager.
- **c**   The fund company.

Answers to this quiz can be found on page 205

2   How can fund shareholders avoid taxes on their mutual fund distributions?

- **a**   Keep their funds in tax-deferred accounts.
- **b**   Reinvest their distributions.
- **c**   Buy funds that have lost money this year.

3   Which type of fund is likely to be the most tax-friendly?

- **a**   A fund that owns high-yielding bonds and has a 50% turnover rate.
- **b**   A fund that owns stocks and has a 50% turnover rate.
- **c**   A fund that owns stocks and has a 10% turnover rate.

4   When is the worst time to buy a fund, from a tax standpoint?

- **a**   Right before a fund makes a distribution.
- **b**   Right after a fund makes a distribution.
- **c**   Any time is a bad time.

5   Which would you rather own in a taxable account?

- **a**   A fund that gives away 5% of its pretax return to taxes.
- **b**   A fund that gives away 15% of its pretax return to taxes.
- **c**   Can't say; it depends which is the better after-tax performer.

Worksheet

What do you think "buying the distribution" means? How can you avoid this trap? What tools might you use? Where would you find them?

On January 1 of last year, your portfolio manager bought 1,000 shares of Microsoft for $80 each. He also bought 2,000 shares of Yahoo at $40 per share. By December 30, Microsoft's share price had climbed to $90 per share and Yahoo's share price hovered at $45. If the manager dumps the stocks, what is the amount of capital gain from those two holdings?

Turnover is the ratio of the trading activity of the fund, expressed in dollars, divided by the total assets in the portfolio, also expressed in dollars.

Here's an example:
Let's say you invest in a mutual fund that has $1 million in assets. If the portfolio manager sells 1,000 shares of Microsoft at $90 per share, the portfolio's trading activity will go up by $90,000. If the manager buys 2,000 shares of Yahoo at $45 per share, the portfolio's activity increases by $90,000. That means that your portfolio has clocked $180,000 in trades. The ratio of those trades to the portfolio's assets is equal to $180,000/ $1,000,000 = 0.18 or 18%!

continued...

Examine your portfolio: Do you own funds with high turnover?
Do you think they have the potential to hurt your overall investment?
Why or why not?

Are the funds in your portfolio likely to be tax-efficient? Why or why not?
Do you hold them in your 401(k) or IRA, or in a taxable account?

Lesson 106: Important Fund Documents

You've seen the advertisements in the papers ("Five Stars!") and the pundits on TV, identifying their hot new pick of the month. And you probably know one or two lucky coworkers who made a mint at some point after taking a chance on some fund or another. But you can't have missed the recent tales about the downfalls of yesterday's favorite fund shops, the management scandals, and the huge, risky bets that cost many investors their retirement dreams.

Clearly, the experience of the last five years suggests that investors need more than performance numbers and hot tips to judge a fund. Before parting with your money, you need to be able to answer questions such as: What is the fund's investment strategy? What are that strategy's risks? How much does the fund cost? How does this fit in with my goals? And who runs the thing, anyway?

In an attempt to restore confidence in America's capital markets, Congress passed the Securities Act and the Securities Exchange Act in 1933 and 1934. These laws were designed to provide more structure and government oversight and to protect investors. The laws required that corporations make truthful public statements and that people who sell and trade securities of any kind deal fairly with investors. These laws set the stage for the birth in 1934 of the Securities and Exchange Commission, a federal agency.

Paper trail

In order to answer these questions you need three valuable fund documents, produced by the company running your mutual fund: the prospectus, the Statement of Additional Information, and the annual report. When you request an information kit from a fund family, you'll usually receive the prospectus and the most recent shareholder report. (Many fund companies also make these documents available on their Web sites.) These documents are packed with legal jargon, convoluted sentences, and boilerplate information in order to fulfill the Securities and Exchange Commission's disclosure requirements and to protect the funds from legal liability. The language can be tremendously intimidating—and reading it is dull work. But these documents are vital for mutual fund investors.

Here's how to get what you need from the prospectus, the Statement of Additional Information, and the annual report.

The Prospectus

The prospectus tells you how to open an account (including minimum-investment requirements), how to purchase or redeem shares, and how to contact shareholder services.

It also details six aspects of the fund that you need to know about before you decide to buy shares.

1. Investment Objective. The investment objective is the mutual fund's purpose. Is the fund seeking to make money over a long-term period? Or is it trying to provide its shareholders regular income each month? If you're investing for your young child's education, you'll want the former. If you're looking for a monthly dividend check, you'll want the latter. But investment objectives are often vague. That's why you'll want to check out the next section.

2. Strategy. The prospectus also describes the types of stocks, bonds, or other securities in which the fund plans to invest. (It does not list the exact stocks that the fund owns, though.) Stock funds spell out what kinds of companies they look for, such as small, fast-growing firms or big, well-established corporations. Bond funds specify what sorts of bonds they generally hold, such as Treasury or corporate bonds. If the fund can invest in foreign securities, the prospectus says so. Most (but not all) restrictions placed on the fund are also mentioned here, including references to short selling, leveraged purchases, and so on.

3. Risks. This section may be the most important part of the prospectus, but it's generally written in very broad language. Every investment has risks associated with it, and a prospectus must explain these risks. For instance, a prospectus for a fund that invests in emerging markets will reveal that the fund is likely to be riskier than a fund that invests in developed countries. Bond-fund prospectuses typically discuss the credit quality of the bonds in the fund's portfolio, as well as how a change in interest rates might affect the value of its holdings.

4. Expenses. It costs money to invest in a mutual fund, and different funds have different fees. A table at the front of every prospectus makes it easy to compare the cost of one fund with another. Here, you'll find the sales commission the fund charges, if any, for buying or selling shares. The prospectus also tells you, in percentage terms, the amount deducted from the fund's return each year to pay for things such as management fees and operational costs.

5. Past Performance. We all know the fund world's catch-all phrase: "Past performance is no guarantee of future results." But a fund's record can give you an idea of how consistent its performance has been. A chart known as the "Financial Highlights" or "Per-Share Data Table" provides the fund's total return for each of the past 10 years, along with some other useful information. It also breaks out the fund's income distributions and provides the year-end NAV.

Some prospectuses include additional return information in the form of a bar chart, which illustrates the fund's calendar-year returns for the past 10 years. This chart is a good way to get a handle on the magnitude of a fund's ups and downs over time. The prospectus may also use a growth of $10,000 graph (also known as a mountain graph, because the peaks and valleys resemble the cross section of a mountain) or a table comparing the fund's performance to indexes or other benchmarks to present return information. (Unless otherwise stated, total return numbers do not take sales charges into account, but they do take into account a fund's annual expense ratio.)

6. Management. The Management section profiles the folks who will be putting your money to work. At this point, many funds identify the name and experience of the fund manager or managers. However, some funds simply list "management team" or some other less-than-helpful phrase. (Beginning in March 2005, however, funds will have to list all of their team members in their prospectuses.)

Also consider the fund manager's tenure—if it's relatively short, the fund's past record may have been achieved under someone else. Find out whether the manager has run other funds in the past. A peek at those funds could give you some clues about the manager's investment style and past success.

Statement of Additional Information

While the prospectus is packed with great information, it shouldn't be your sole source of data on a fund. A fund's Statement of Additional Information (SAI) contains more great tidbits about the fund's inner workings. You'll generally have to request this document by calling the fund company: Funds send out prospectuses and annual reports as a matter of routine, but SAIs are often considered second-tier documents.

Fund families may consider SAIs secondary, but these statements usually provide far more detail than the prospectus about what the fund can and cannot invest in. Further, this document usually identifies just who represents your interests on the fund's board of directors—and just how much you pay them for their efforts and how much these directors own of the fund.

Finally, you can find more details about your fund's expenses here. Shareholders in Putnam Fund for Growth and Income wouldn't know they shelled out $28 million in brokerage fees in 2001 unless they had read the fund's SAI. SAIs also break down where 12b-1 fees go, if the fund charges them. (These are fees that the fund can use for marketing, rewarding brokers, and attracting more investors.) For example, Legg Mason Value Trust spent $49 million of the $96 million in 12b-1 fees it collected in 2002 compensating brokers for selling the fund. It's your money; you should know where it's going.

The Shareholder Report

A mutual fund's shareholder report is part biography, part blueprint, and part ledger book.

A good shareholder report is like a biography in that it sets out what happened to the fund over the past quarter, six months, or year, and why. It's like a blueprint because it sets before you all the investments—stocks, bonds, and other securities—that the fund has made. And it's like a ledger book because it discloses a fund's costs, profits, and many other financial facts. Mutual funds are required by the SEC to release a shareholder report at least twice a year, though some fund families publish them quarterly.

Not all of the following items are required by law to appear in a mutual fund's shareholder report. The SEC allows some of the information to be included in other documents, such as a fund's prospectus or Statement of Additional Information. However, a good report will contain all of the elements discussed below.

Letter from the President

Typically, the first item you'll find in a shareholder report is a letter from the president of the company that advises or manages your fund. The best letters will contain straightforward, useful discussions of the economic trends that have affected the markets during the past 6 or 12 months and provides some context for evaluating your fund. Poor letters, in contrast, will discuss anything but the current financial climate and the performance of the fund family's offerings.

Some companies are known for great shareholder letters. Third Avenue Value's Marty Whitman writes exemplary shareholder letters every three months. In these letters, he describes which stocks he and his team sold, bought, or left alone, and why. The Vanguard Group's shareholder letters are also noteworthy for their sector overviews. Because many of the shop's funds are index offerings, they rarely spend much time on individual holdings, but their industry analysis is always worth a look.

Top shareholder letters

Letter from the Portfolio Manager

This is a fund-specific examination of the recent performance—and therefore much more important to you as a fund shareholder. Well-written shareholder letters discuss individual stocks that the fund owns and the industries in which the fund invested. A good manager letter will also explain what broad market trends might have fueled or hindered your fund's performance. Finally, most managers will give you an indication of what you can expect from the fund in the future, given an unchanged strategy.

Investors should demand a lot from shareholder letters, particularly in times of declining performance. If shareholder reports leave your questions unanswered, let your mutual fund company know. (Note: Many fund companies have begun sending out portfolio-manager letters that are separate from their shareholder reports, rather than bundling them together.)

Recent Fund Performance

The portfolio manager's report is generally followed by a discussion of recent performance. The report should compare your fund's performance to both a benchmark, such as the S&P 500 Index (the standard benchmark for large-company stock funds) or the Russell 2000 Index (for small-company funds), as well as to the average performance of funds with similar investment strategies.

When evaluating your fund's performance, be sure that the benchmark the fund chooses is appropriate for its style. For example, a technology fund shouldn't compare itself to the S&P 500 and nothing else; it should measure its performance against a technology benchmark.

In addition to benchmark comparison, the report should give you an idea of how the fund has performed over various time frames, both short and long term.

Portfolio Holdings

Funds often list the portfolio's largest holdings and provide some information about what these companies do or why the manager owns them. Some reports will also indicate, via a pie chart or table, the sectors in which the fund is heavily invested.

This general overview is complemented by a complete list of the fund's portfolio holdings—including stocks, bonds, and cash—as of the date of the report. These holdings are usually segmented by industry. (Foreign funds may segment by country.) While you might not recognize all the names of the stocks in the portfolio, this listing is useful if you're wondering whether the fund is holding many names in one industry or making a few large selected bets.

Footnotes

Don't forget to read the fine print. In the footnotes, you can find out if fund managers are practicing such strategies as shorting stocks or hedging exposure to foreign currency, which can significantly affect the fund's performance.

Footnotes can also provide insights into particular portfolio holdings. For instance, the footnotes of Baron Asset's December 31, 2001, report revealed that the fund held substantial enough positions in some stocks that they were deemed "affiliates." Other stocks were noted as illiquid securities and 144A securities, which means they're more difficult to trade than plain common stocks.

Financial Statements

A fund's annual report concludes with its financial statements. Brace yourself: There's a lot of data here. In fact, this is where we get a lot of the data for the fund data reports shown on Morningstar.com and, if we do say so ourselves, we do a pretty good job of clarifying that data and putting it into context.

However, if raw numbers are your thing, you should take a look at the following: First, examine what's known as the fund's Selected Per-Share Data. This is usually the last page of actual information, located just before the legal discussion of accounting practices. Here you'll find the fund's NAVs, expense ratios, and portfolio turnover ratios for each of the past five years (or more). Check to see if the fund's expense ratio has gone down over time (we hope it has) and whether its turnover rate has changed much (if so, you may want to find out why).

Cost-conscious investors can check out the breakdown of a fund's expenses, including management fees, under the Statement of Operations. In addition, you can find out how much in unrealized or undistributed capital gains you're facing, using the Statement of Assets and Liabilities. (A gain is unrealized when a stock has gone up but the fund hasn't sold it. As soon as the fund sells the stock, it becomes a "realized" gain, which has to be distributed to shareholders. We explored this concept in Lesson 105.)

What to Do Next

You can request a prospectus, SAI, or annual report by phone, by direct mail, and sometimes by e-mail. Many funds also make this literature available for download at their Web sites. All mutual funds file their prospectuses, shareholder reports, and SAIs with the SEC. You can view these at the SEC's Web site: www.sec.gov.

Obviously, annual reports and shareholder letters may not have all the details you're looking for. While mutual fund shops aren't always forthcoming, some companies have gone the distance when it comes to staying in touch with shareholders. A particularly impressive series of articles appears on Pacific Investment Management Company's Web site, penned by the shop's bond managers. In the spring of 2004, PIMCO's top brass responded promptly to concerns about mutual fund scandals, publishing a series of letters to shareholders on the shop's Web site.

When it comes to communication, less is not more

While we suggest that you begin your fund evaluation with these documents, we don't think you should stop there. Seek out third-party sources, such as Morningstar, to help put your fund into context. Compare it with other funds that have similar investment approaches. You should evaluate how its costs stack up, if its performance is competitive, and if it compensates for the risks it is taking on.

Fearless Facts

▶ A complete prospectus will include the investment objective, an introduction to just what kind of an investment you have on your
hands. It's full of fairly vague terms, but favorites include "long-term
holding" (usually a modest-growth fund) or "conservative"
(often referring to a fund with a value-oriented strategy). You won't
get much from this section, but it's a start.

▶ If you're interested in performance, Shareholder Reports are truly the
meat of the matter.

▶ The President's Letter is quite general; if you're pressed for time, this
is often the one section you can afford to skip.

▶ The Manager's Letter should include an explanation of just what
went down in the period covered by the Report. Look for the following:

  ▸ An explanation of over- or underperformance relative to a
  relevant peer group or benchmark.

  ▸ Company-specific information that might help explain strong or
  weak results.

  ▸ Future plans for the portfolio.

▶ The footnotes will have details on unusual strategies that the fund
manager is using (such as hedging currencies or shorting stocks).
After five years of corporate scandal and intrigue, all investors should
know just how important footnotes can be!

Quiz

1 Which of the following appears in all prospectuses?

> **a** The names of all portfolio managers.
>
> **b** The names of the board of directors.
>
> **c** Management fees.

Answers to this quiz can be found on page 206

2 The Investment Objective portion of the prospectus is most helpful in determining:

> **a** What the fund's general purpose is.
>
> **b** What type of securities the fund owns.
>
> **c** What sort of risks are associated with the fund.

3 For details about how your fund fees are spent, consult the:

> **a** Prospectus.
>
> **b** Statement of Additional Information.
>
> **c** Neither.

4 Where in the shareholder report are you most likely to find an explanation of why your fund performed the way it did during the past year?

> **a** In the President's Letter.
>
> **b** In the Portfolio Manager's Letter.
>
> **c** In the footnotes.

5 Turn to the Per-Share Data for:

> **a** The turnover ratio.
>
> **b** A list of what stocks the fund owns.
>
> **c** A breakdown of expenses in dollar terms.

Worksheet

If you have the prospectus for one of your funds, it's time to pull it out. If not, go online and find a prospectus for a fund you're interested in. (Most fund companies let you download a free prospectus from their Web sites.)

Find the fund's investment objective. What is it? Does it fit with your own investment goals?

What is the fund's investment strategy?

What are the risks associated with that strategy?

Who's running the fund? How long has the current manager (or management team) been in place?

Is your fund sold through advisors only, or can individual investors buy it without paying a sales charge, or load?

continued...

Does the fund charge a redemption fee if you redeem your shares within a certain period of time? Why do you think a fund might charge such a fee?

Fearlessly Select the
Best Funds

Lesson 107: How to Purchase a Fund

Investing in a mutual fund may seem tremendously overwhelming at first. Instead of choosing just one company and one stock (one price, one ticker, one exchange, etc.), you're suddenly charged with committing to a whole portfolio, choosing an investment approach, monitoring someone else's record, and getting to know a whole new vocabulary. Before you get mired in those details, you need to decide whether you want some help choosing your funds or whether you'd rather do it on your own. Like most everything in life, both paths have benefits and drawbacks.

Want Some Help?

Maybe you don't have the time or interest to design your own mutual fund portfolio. Fine! All sorts of financial advisors, from planners to brokers, can help you pull together a financial plan and a basket of funds that can help you achieve your goals.

Of course, this service isn't free. If you work with an advisor, you might pay an up-front fee of some sort, perhaps a percentage of your investment money. Or your advisor may forgo a fee and earn a commission by investing your money in what are called load funds. A load, or sales charge, is deducted from your investment when you buy or sell shares, depending on the fee structure. This load is used to compensate the advisor for selling you the fund. (Note that the load does not go to the fund manager; he or she receives another fee, called the management fee, which we've discussed in Lesson 104.) Some advisors are fee- and commission-based, which means they'll charge you some combination of the two.

The advantages of working with an advisor are clear: You have someone helping you make financial decisions, taking care of paperwork for you, monitoring fund performance, and forcing you to stick to your investment plan for tomorrow instead of cashing in for an around-the-world jaunt today.

The drawbacks include cost, of course. There's also the challenge of finding an advisor with whom you work well, someone you can trust to put your interests before his or her own, and who will turn your financial dreams into realities, not nightmares. Further, you want to find an advisor who is willing to take the time to teach you about investing and about what he or she is doing with your portfolio. It's your money, after all, and you need to understand why it's invested the way it is.

Go It Alone, Version 1

Those with the time and interest to learn about investing and to monitor their own portfolios can invest in funds without the help of an advisor. If you choose to invest on your own, focus on no-load funds, which do not charge any sales commissions. Why pay a commission if you're not getting any investment advice in return?

Go-it-alone types can buy funds directly from no-load fund groups (also called fund families) such as Fidelity, Vanguard, and T. Rowe Price. (Fidelity runs load funds, too.) To buy a fund from a fund family, request an application from the fund group by calling its 800 number. You can find these numbers on Morningstar.com's fund data reports. Most fund families provide prospectuses and applications on their Web sites, as well.

New investors who plan to buy more than one fund might choose one of the larger no-load families. Why? Because these families are diversified: They offer stock and bond funds, domestic and international funds, and large- and small-company funds. Take it from us: Most fund investors eventually own more than one fund because of the need for diversification; by investing with one of the major fund families, you can easily transfer assets from one fund to another.

Investing with a single fund family—even a large one—can be limiting, though. For example, some families don't offer a wide array of funds. Take the Janus Funds, for example. The group specializes in large-company growth investing, but the company offers very few bond funds of any kind.

Another way to diversify, then, is to invest with several fund families, a series of specialists who do one thing particularly well. You could buy a large-company growth fund from, say, Janus, a small-company fund from Royce Funds, a bond fund from PIMCO, and an international fund from Tweedy, Browne. But that would mean a lot of paperwork; each family would send you separate account and tax statements. If you own more than a few funds, the paperwork can become maddening.

Go It Alone, Version 2

Do-it-yourselfers who hate paperwork but want a lot of choices shouldn't despair: No-transaction fee networks, also known as "supermarkets," are a popular solution. Charles Schwab pioneered this idea in 1992 when it launched the Schwab OneSource program. If you invest through OneSource, you can choose from thousands of funds offered by dozens of fund families—and there's no direct cost to you. So you could buy one fund from Janus, another from Royce, yet another from PIMCO, and one from Tweedy, Browne, and receive all of your information about performance, taxes, etc., on one consolidated statement.

| Buyer beware | Supermarkets can be appealing, but make sure you read the fine print. Some supermarkets charge a transaction fee to buy funds that aren't part of an "NTF plan." (NTF stands for "no transaction fee.") And those transaction fees can add up, especially if you're investing small amounts (and let's be honest: many of us who frequent supermarkets are small-time investors). The charge is usually a flat fee, so if you're investing a small amount—say $100 or $500—and the transaction fee is $35, that's a huge portion of your investment. This can be particularly damaging if you want to build your investments by dollar-cost averaging (investing a small amount every month). |

There are a number of fund supermarkets today, and more and more fund families are getting into the act: T. Rowe Price, Vanguard, and Fidelity have supermarkets that include funds outside of those families.

What could the drawbacks here possibly be? Surprisingly, one drawback is cost. While it is true that fund supermarkets do not charge you when you invest in a fund through their programs, they charge the fund companies to be included in their programs. That charge ranges from 0.25% to 0.40% of assets per year. As any student of economics knows, that fee acts a whole lot like a tax and it's passed right along to shareholders—that's right, to you—as part of a fund's expense ratio, the fee the fund charges you each year for managing your money. The real kicker is that shareholders are paying these fees whether they buy the funds through the fund supermarket or directly from the fund family.

Some observers, including Vanguard founder Jack Bogle, also suggest that fund supermarkets encourage rapid trading among funds. Most supermarkets offer online trading, and with so many funds from so many families investing in so many different things to choose from, the temptation is great. But trading too much can hurt your portfolio's overall performance. (We'll tackle that subject in depth in a later lesson.)

A note about speed

In an era of instant communication, you'll notice that a lot of online brokerage services use speed as a big selling point, suggesting that traditional relationships with the mutual fund company or a face-to-face relationship with an advisor are not only relics of the past, but dangerously old-fashioned. But it's not clear whether investors get faster service through a brokerage account; if they do, it offers marginal benefits.

First, a lot of mutual fund companies allow you to buy and sell your funds online these days, just like the big supermarkets or online brokerage firms. And even if you can't conduct the transaction online, you can always call the fund company. Either way, it shouldn't matter much. After all, fund transactions only occur at the close of business for that day. So whether you call your fund company at 10:00 a.m. to buy one of their funds or make the purchase over the Internet at 12:30 p.m., your transaction should take place at the end of the day. In addition, immediacy isn't usually critical when buying and selling open-end mutual funds. Let's say something bad happens to your fund: The superstar manager quits in a huff. The fund isn't going to plummet 50% in a day just because the manager left. It can't because the fund's NAV—its daily "price"—is simply a reflection of the value of the fund's underlying securities.

Fearless Facts

▶ There's something for everyone when it comes to mutual fund investing.

▶ For organized do-it-yourselfers: Try building a mutual fund portfolio using funds from one of the industry's largest no-load fund shops, such as Vanguard, Fidelity, or T. Rowe Price.

▶ For do-it-yourselfers who want more variety: Consolidate your portfolio at one location, using one of the fund supermarkets that have made a name for themselves in the past 10 years, such as Charles Schwab. A few large fund shops run these supermarkets too, allowing investors to invest in funds from other companies.

▶ For those seeking some hand-holding: Advisors can work with you on some or all of your portfolio. You could, for example, simply discuss your child's college fund with an advisor or you could get advice on all your investments.

▶ If you're going to hold hands, it's vital that you do your research. Ask your friends or consult financial Web sites including www.morningstar.com!

▶ Remember that you'll always pay a fee when you work with an advisor. We'll explore different fee structures in future lessons.

Quiz

1   Which answer is not a way financial advisors are compensated?

> a   A percentage of your investment money.
>
> b   A part of the fund manager's fee.
>
> c   A commission on your mutual funds.

Answers to this quiz can be found on page 206

2   When you buy a load fund through an advisor, where does the load that you pay go?

> a   Into the fund.
>
> b   To the fund manager.
>
> c   To your advisor.

3   If you are a go-it-alone investor, avoid:

> a   Load funds.
>
> b   No-load funds.
>
> c   Funds sold through a fund supermarket.

4   No-transaction fee networks charge:

> a   Up-front charges to investors who invest through them.
>
> b   Sales charges to investors who sell through them.
>
> c   Fund companies for being part of the network.

5   Investing with one of the more diverse fund families or a fund supermarket:

> a   Limits your paper work.
>
> b   Limits your diversification options.
>
> c   Makes trading more difficult.

Worksheet

If you own mutual funds, how did you invest in them? Through a broker or financial advisor? Directly through the fund family? Through your 401(k)? Through a supermarket such as Charles Schwab?

What are the advantages of using a financial advisor? Should loads play a role in your decision to invest through an advisor?

Why might you choose to invest through a major fund family such as Fidelity or Vanguard?

What are some drawbacks of using a fund supermarket?
Some observers, including Vanguard founder Jack Bogle, suggest that supermarkets encourage rapid trading in and out of funds.
How might that sort of trading affect long-term investors in a fund?

Lesson 108: Methods for Investing in Mutual Funds

It's hard enough to decide whether or not to invest with an advisor and to commit to a mutual fund style or portfolio goal. In addition, you have to decide how much you want to invest in a fund, and when.

If you're fortunate enough to have money to invest, you'll need to choose one of the following approaches:

1 Wait to invest your jackpot until your favorite fund cools off or heats up.
2 Invest the entire wad immediately.
3 Put a little bit to work at a time.

You should be aware that the route you choose can have a profound impact on your return.

Waiting, or Market-Timing

Let's start with the first route, holding off on an investment until you sense the time is right. That can mean when the fund's performance falls, when it rises, or when the moon is full on an odd-numbered day of the week in a month beginning with J. Such a strategy is often called market-timing.

As you can probably sense, we're not keen on market-timing. Evidence suggests that it just doesn't work. Predicting the future has never been easy—just ask anyone who has had his or her fortune told. Further, studies from Morningstar have shown that investors' timing often leaves something to be desired—they buy in when a fund is ready to cool off and sell when its performance is ready to pick up. And even if you make the "right" market call, the mutual fund world usually doesn't reward you in a dramatic enough way to make the risk worth it.

Chalk it up to the cruelty of mathematics, as illustrated in an experiment conducted by Morningstar. We went back 20 years and assumed that in each quarter, an investor chose to own all stocks (represented by the s&p 500) or all cash (in our experiment, Treasury bills). A market-timer who picked the better performer half the time still ended up way behind the market after two decades. We found that not until the timer's hit rate reached 65% did he beat the s&p 500. In other words, the market-timer had to be right two out of three times to justify the effort.

This is largely because over time, the stock market has notched higher gains than holding cash. Botching a market-timing decision usually means sacrificing good performance. Worse still, missing a period of strong returns means giving up the chance to make even more on those strong returns, thanks to the effects of compounding. (That is, each year you earn returns on the returns you earned in prior years, as well as on your initial investment.)

Investing All at Once, or Lump-Sum Investing

If market-timing is a losing strategy, what about the opposite: putting all the money to work at once? Many financial advisors recommend this approach above the others because the market goes up more often than it goes down.

Here's an example: Say you decide to invest an amount of $10,000 all at once in one fund while your friend, who also happens to have $10,000 to invest, instead places $2,000 per month in the same fund over the next five months. The fund consistently rises in value during that time. The chart below illustrates what would happen to the two investments.

Dollar-Cost Averaging vs. Lump-Sum Investing when Fund Value Increases

	Price Per Share	Your Friend's Investment $2,000 buys	Your Investment $10,000 buys
Month 1	$1.80	1,111 shares	5,556 shares
Month 2	$1.82	1,099 shares	—
Month 3	$1.85	1,081 shares	—
Month 4	$1.87	1,070 shares	—
Month 5	$1.90	1,053 shares	—
	Total Shares	5,414	5,556
	Ending Value	$10,287	$10,556

You would end up ahead because you own more shares at the end of the five-month period. And you own more shares because, due to the consistently rising value of the fund, your friend couldn't afford to purchase as many shares as you had purchased originally. But what happens if the value of your fund fluctuates dramatically during those five months?

Dollar-Cost Averaging vs. Lump-Sum Investing when Fund Value Fluctuates

	Price Per Share	Your Friend's Investment $2,000 buys	Your Investment $10,000 buys
Month 1	$1.80	1,111 shares	5,556 shares
Month 2	$1.20	1,667 shares	—
Month 3	$1.85	1,081 shares	—
Month 4	$1.35	1,481 shares	—
Month 5	$1.90	1,053 shares	—
Total Shares		6,393	5,556
Ending Value		$12,147	$10,556

In this case, your friend ends up in the lead. By investing a fixed dollar amount in the fund every month, your friend bought more shares when the price was low, fewer shares when the price was high, and ended up with more shares after five months.

To be sure, such drastic fluctuations in NAV are rare. Because the stock market generally goes up more often than it goes down, most investors will receive the best long-term results by lump-sum investing.

Why Dollar-Cost Average?

Investing in dribs and drabs may not be the path to greater return, but we still think dollar-cost averaging, or investing a set amount on

a regular basis, is a great method of investing. Incidentally, if you contribute to a 401(K) plan at work, you're already investing this way.

Our argument for dollar-cost averaging has a couple of dimensions.
First, dollar-cost averaging can reduce risk. If your mutual fund
declines in value, the worth of your investment is less, even though
you still own the same number of shares. In the same way that dollar-cost averaging will net you more shares in a declining market, it
can curtail your losses as the fund goes down. The chart below illustrates this point.

Dollar-Cost Averaging vs. Lump-Sum Investing when Fund Value Decreases

	Price Per Share	Your Friend's Investment $2,000 buys	Your Investment $10,000 buys
Month 1	$1.80	1,111 shares	5,556 shares
Month 2	$1.60	1,250 shares	—
Month 3	$1.45	1,379 shares	—
Month 4	$1.30	1,538 shares	—
Month 5	$1.20	1,667 shares	—
Total Shares		6,945	5,556
Ending Value		$8,334	$6,667

In this example, both you and your friend lost money (remember,
you each started with $10,000), but your friend lost less by dollar-cost
averaging. She had cash sitting on the sidelines that did not lose
value. And when the fund rebounds, your friend will also be in better shape because she owns more shares of the fund than you do.

The second reason we like dollar-cost averaging is that it instills discipline. Investors often chase past returns, buying funds after a hot performance streak. And they'll sell funds when returns slow or decline. Bad idea: That's a form of market-timing. But dollar-cost averaging prevents you from market-timing because you're buying all the time. Heck, you may even forget that you're investing if you set up an automatic-investment plan with a mutual fund family.

Which leads us to the final reason we love dollar-cost averaging: It's a crafty way to invest in some great mutual funds that might be inaccessible otherwise. Many fund companies will waive their minimum initial investment requirement if you agree to set up an automatic-investment plan and invest a little each month or quarter.

Got $100?	A little extra money can go a long way if you're willing to commit it to an automatic-investment plan. Below you'll find a list of fund complexes where you can start constructing diversified portfolios by investing a small amount of money each month.			
	American Funds	$50	MFS Investment Management	$50
	Putnam Investments	$25	Dreyfus	$100
	AIM Distributors	$50	USAA Group	$50
	T. Rowe Price	$100	TIAA-CREF	$25

Decision Time

While market-timing is out of the question for all investors (but some still try), whether you invest all at once or a little at a time depends on how much time you have to invest and whether your primary goal is maximizing return or minimizing risk.

Remember: This is one of the areas in which there are no hard and fast rules. In a volatile market environment, dollar-cost averaging is likely to work better than lump-sum investing. However, when markets are on the up and up, lump-sum investors are going to look pretty smart.	The rules don't always apply

The shorter your time horizon, the greater chance you take of losing money with a lump-sum investment. However, if you had $20,000 to invest, it probably wouldn't make much sense to invest $1,000 per year for the next 20 years. Over long time frames, funds go up more often than they go down, and when they go down, they eventually bounce back. It is almost certain that the NAV you would pay 10 years from now would be higher than the NAV you would pay today.

We suggest combining the two strategies: Invest as much as you can today and vow to invest a little more each month or quarter. That'll keep you disciplined and have you investing right away.

Fearless Facts

▶ History suggests that market-timing—attempting to invest when the market is due for an upswing and sell before it heads down—simply doesn't pay off. Over time, the opportunity cost of a missed call can be fairly substantial.

▶ Dollar-cost averaging reduces risk. If your investment drops, dollar-cost averaging will curtail your losses. That's because it lessens the risk that you will invest a big lump sum of money at exactly the wrong time.

▶ Dollar-cost averaging also encourages discipline. If you're on a set schedule, you can't chase hot returns and you can't flee when the market turns rough.

▶ Finally, dollar-cost averaging may allow you to invest in funds with high minimum investments that might be closed to you otherwise. In other words, high-minimum funds will sometimes let you in as long as you're willing to commit to them.

Quiz

1   To successfully outperform the market by timing, Morningstar found that investors' calls must be right:

Answers to this quiz can be found on page 207

a   Half of the time.

b   Two-thirds of the time.

c   All of the time.

2   If a fund's value increases every month for a 12-month period, who most likely comes out ahead?

a   The market-timer.

b   The lump-sum investor.

c   The dollar-cost-averaging investor.

3   If a stock fund was very volatile over a 12-month period, who most likely comes out ahead?

a   The market-timer.

b   The lump-sum investor.

c   The dollar-cost-averaging investor.

4   Which is false? Dollar-cost averaging:

a   Always leads to better returns than lump-sum investing.

b   Instills discipline.

c   Allows you to invest in some funds that might otherwise be off-limits.

5   If you have a 10-year time horizon to invest, what would Morningstar say is the best approach?

a   Lump-sum investing.

b   Dollar-cost averaging.

c   Both.

Worksheet

Examine your investment style over the past few years. Which category does it fall into?

◯ Market-timing ◯ Lump-sum investing ◯ Dollar-cost averaging

Why have you invested that way? Do you think you'll invest that way in the future?

Do you think your investment style has helped or hurt your portfolio's returns over the long term?

In a steadily rising market environment, such as the one that many of us remember in the late 1990s, which investment approach likely worked better most of the time: lump-sum investing or dollar-cost averaging? Why?

continued...

Compare the following two options, assuming your dividends are not reinvested:

Option A: You decide to invest $600 per month in a mutual fund using an automatic-investment account and the money is pulled straight from your paycheck on the same day each month. After a while, you hardly know it's gone. If a share of the fund costs $50 in October, your $600 will buy 12 shares. If the price rises to $75 in November, you buy eight shares. If the price drops to $25 in December, you buy 24 shares and so on.

Option B: You decide to invest $1,800 at the beginning of October in one lump-sum payment to the same mutual fund.

NAV of fund	Value of Option A	Value of Option B
October: $50	12 Shares @ $50 ea.	36 Shares @ $50 ea.
November: $75	8 Shares @ $75 ea.	—
December: $25	24 Shares @ $25 ea.	—
January: $50	12 Shares @ $50 ea.	—
Ending value:		

Which strategy yields a higher return by the end of January?
What market environment hurts this strategy?

Lesson 109: Five Questions to Ask Before Buying a Mutual Fund

You may feel intimidated by the task of picking a mutual fund. With more than 15,000 funds to choose from, it's tempting to buy a magazine or visit a Web site that will tell you exactly which funds you should buy, or to just pick the fund that's topping the performance charts.

These aren't the best ways to find the fund that will meet your goals or suit your investment personality, however. The next section will give you a better idea of how to approach the vast marketplace for mutual funds and will introduce five questions that you need to ask and answer before buying any stock fund.

1 How has it performed?
2 How risky has it been?
3 What does it own?
4 Who runs it?
5 What does it cost?

These questions form the foundation of Morningstar's approach to fund selection. We'll address these questions in depth in subsequent lessons, but here's a taste of what's to come.

How Has It Performed?

Many would say that a fund that produced returns of 22% per year for the past five years has a better manager than a fund that returned 20% per year over the same period. That's sometimes the case but not always. The fund that gained 20% may have beaten competing funds that follow the same investment style by six percentage points, while the 22% gainer may have lagged its competitors by a mile.

To really know how well a fund is doing, put a fund's returns into context. Compare the fund's returns to appropriate benchmarks—to indexes and to other funds that invest in the same types of securities.

How Risky Has It Been?

Of course, the very act of investing involves an element of risk. After all, you're choosing to give your money to a portfolio manager rather than socking it away under the bed or putting it into a savings account at your local bank.

Generally, the greater the return of an investment, the greater the risk—and therefore the greater potential for loss. Investors who take on a lot of risk expect a greater return from their investments, but they don't always get it. Other investors are willing to give up the potential for large gains in return for a more probable return. Consider a fund's volatility in conjunction with the returns it produces. Two funds with equal returns might not be equally attractive investments; one could be far more volatile than the other.

Inside the Star Rating

Time Frame	Morningstar Return	Morningstar Risk	Morningstar Rating
3-year	Above Average	Average	★★★★
5-year	High	Average	★★★★★
10-year	High	Average	★★★★★
Overall	High	Average	★★★★★

American Funds Growth Fund of America has produced high returns with only average risk, earning it Morningstar's 5-star rating. The rating is comprised of a weighted average of ratings from three-, five-, and 10-year periods.

There are a number of ways to measure how volatile a fund is. There are four main risk measurements that appear in mutual fund shareholder reports, in the financial media, and on Morningstar.com. These include standard deviation, beta, Morningstar risk ratings, and Morningstar bear market rankings. It's also helpful to check out a fund's quarterly and annual returns in different market conditions to get a sense for its potential volatility.

What Does It Own?

To set realistic expectations for what a fund can do for you, it's important to know what kinds of securities a fund's manager buys: Stocks? Bonds? Both? These broad asset classes have different characteristics, so you shouldn't expect them to perform in a similar manner. For example, most investors wouldn't hope for a 10% gain from a bond fund, but that kind of return isn't an unrealistic expectation for certain stock funds.

Unfortunately, you can't rely on a fund's name to tell you what it owns. Fidelity Magellan is a giant in the fund industry, but its moniker gives you very little idea of the types of securities its manager buys.

As we mentioned earlier, fund managers can buy just stocks, just bonds, or a combination of the two. They can stick with U.S. companies or venture abroad. They can hold popular big companies, such as Coca-Cola or Gillette, or focus on small companies most of us have never heard of. They can load up on high-priced companies that are growing quickly, or they can favor value stocks with lower earnings prospects but cheap prices. Finally, managers can own 20 or 200 stocks. How a manager chooses to invest your money is one of the most important factors that will drive performance.

To get a feel for how a manager invests, examine a fund's portfolio. The financial statements published by the mutual fund company always disclose this information. You can also access portfolio data, including top holdings, sector breakdowns, and the Morningstar style box (which we'll explore in later lessons) on Morningstar.com and other Web sites.

Do your homework	More than 15,000 funds to choose from and no idea how to begin? Start with research. There are hundreds of educational Web sites to choose from, including Morningstar, Yahoo Finance, and the SEC's Web site. Moreover, many mutual fund companies now offer educational materials on their sites. (Vanguard's site is first-rate.) Keep in mind that you're under no obligation to buy.

Who Runs It?

Mutual funds are only as good as the people behind them: the fund managers who make the investment decisions. Because the fund manager is the person most responsible for a fund's performance, it's important to know who calls the shots for your mutual fund—as well as how long he or she has been doing it. Make sure that the manager who built the majority of the fund's record is still the one in charge. Otherwise, you may be in for an unpleasant surprise. We'll return to the issue of fund management later.

What Does It Cost?

As we pointed out in Lesson 104, mutual funds aren't free. You should pay for professional money management if you need it, but paying enormous expenses to invest is like giving money away. That's because every penny that you give to fund management or to brokerage commissions is a penny you take away from your own return. Further, costs are one of the few constants in investing: They'll remain pretty stable year in and year out while the returns of stocks and bonds will fluctuate. You can't control the whims of the market, but you can control how much you pay for your mutual funds.

Unfortunately, fund costs are somewhat invisible, buried in shareholder reports and taken right off the top of your fund data. Morningstar provides a detailed breakdown of a fund's costs in the Fees and Expenses section of its Fund Report on Morningstar.com.

Fearless Facts

▶ This is a section with a lot of "musts." Investing takes discipline and work. This section introduces you to the ground rules.

▶ Remember: Similar performance doesn't mean similar funds. Two funds may look a lot alike in terms of returns, risk, or even top portfolio holdings. But it's only in considering all of these factors together that you get a true sense of what the fund is—and isn't.

▶ No excuses. You absolutely must know the following about every single one of your funds:
1. How has it performed?
2. How risky has it been?
3. What does it own?
4. Who runs it?
5. What does it cost?

▶ You can find the answers to the preceding questions on the fund shop's Web site, by calling its 800 number, by perusing fund shareholder reports, or—the easy way—by checking its Fund Report on Morningstar.com.

▶ The most important lesson that you've learned in this section? There is no free ride. Funds that boast larger returns always go hand-in-hand with greater risk. Period.

Quiz

1 How can you gauge how competitive a fund's returns are?

Answers to this quiz can be found on page 208

a   Look at a fund's return in isolation.

b   Compare a fund's return with those of an appropriate benchmark.

c   Compare a fund's return with its standard deviation.

2 If Fund A returns an average of 25% per year and Fund B earns 15% per year:

a   Fund A likely has a greater potential for loss.

b   Fund B likely has a greater potential for loss.

c   Fund A is the better choice for all investors.

3 What's the best way to get a feel for how a fund manager invests?

a   Look at the fund's name.

b   Check out its list of holdings and the sectors in which it invests.

c   Compare the fund's performance with a benchmark's.

4 Who decides exactly which securities a mutual fund owns?

a   You, the shareholder.

b   The mutual fund company.

c   The fund manager.

5 What's the most important thing to know about your fund managers?

a   How much their funds return each year.

b   How they manage the fund.

c   How much their salary is.

Worksheet

For this worksheet, pull out the latest shareholder report of your favorite fund. If you don't have one handy, you can go online and find a shareholder report on a major fund company's Web site.

First, flip to the details on the fund's portfolio. Where is your fund investing? Stocks? Bonds? Is it heavily concentrated in a few holdings or spread out? Does your fund have heavy exposure in a few industries, or is it spread out across many different kinds of industries? Is it investing abroad?

Examine the fund's performance. What are its returns over the past one, three, and five years? How does this compare with its peers or category average? Is it outperforming a relevant benchmark?

Look at your fund's expenses for the most recent fiscal year. Is its expense amount higher or lower than in the previous year?

Read the manager's discussion of how the fund has performed. Is the manager being forthright about what went right and what went wrong? Why do you think this might be important?

Lesson 110: Why Knowing Your Fund Manager Matters

Everyone remembers the glory days of Notre Dame football. In the late 1980s and early 1990s, under the watch of head coach Lou Holtz, the Fighting Irish team was a college powerhouse to be reckoned with. During his 11-season tenure, Holtz boasted an admirable .765 winning percentage and led the Irish to a national championship in 1988 (and fell just shy of capturing the crown in 1989 and 1993).

But all good things must come to an end. Holtz left in 1997. His replacement, Bob Davie, was never able to find his groove as the Irish spun to a virtually unheard of 25 losses during his five-year stint.

Fund investors can learn something from this reversal of fortune. Like college football teams, mutual funds are only as good as the people behind them: the fund managers. Portfolio managers are the people who decide what to buy and what to sell, and when. Because the fund manager is the person who is most responsible for a fund's performance, knowing who's calling the shots and for how long is key to smart mutual-fund-picking.

The Morningstar.com Fund Reports include a management section that details each fund's management history. Although they are required to file this information with the SEC, some fund companies continue to be a bit cagey about who, exactly, is running their funds and when. That's why it's best to check an independent source for details of manager tenure.

Seeking tenure

Different Manager Structures

Before discussing further why managers are important, let's step back and examine the three ways in which funds can be managed.

First, there's the single-manager approach. In this setup, there's one person who takes primary responsibility for making the fund's investment decisions. The manager doesn't do all the research, trading, and decision making without help from others, though. For example, Robert Stansky is still listed as the sole manager of Fidelity Magellan, but Fidelity's analysts feed him plenty of stock ideas. The single manager is sole decision maker, not the sole idea generator.

Second, there's the management team, popularized by families such as American Century, Scudder, and Putnam. Here, two or more people work together to choose stocks. The level of one team member's involvement or responsibilities can be tough to gauge, though. Sometimes there's a lead manager who is the final arbiter (as with some Scudder funds), while other times it is more of a democracy (as with Dodge & Cox).

Third, and most rare, there is the multiple-manager system. The fund's assets are divided among a number of managers who work independently of each other. American Funds is the biggest fund family using this approach. Multiple managers are more common with funds managed by firms other than the fund company itself, such as Vanguard Windsor II, the CDC Nvest funds, and the American Aadvantage group. In all of those cases, the fund company hires managers from several other companies to run the fund.

Why Managers Matter

We think it is always important to know who a fund's manager is, whether the fund is run by one person or a whole team. Equally important is how long the person or team has been running the fund. Make sure that the manager who built the majority of the fund's record is still the one in charge. Otherwise, you may be in for a surprise.

Take Guardian Park Avenue. In April 1998, longtime manager Chuck Albers left the fund. Albers had compiled an excellent record: The fund was one of the top-performing, large-blend funds for the trailing 10 years. But the fund wasn't the same after Albers left. It went on to badly lag the average large-blend fund during the next few years. Investors who bought the fund based on its long-term record, but who didn't realize the person who built that record had moved on, were sorely disappointed.

When funds have a lot of flexibility and a somewhat complicated strategy, the skill of the manager is key. For example, Excelsior Value and Restructuring usually picks up beaten-down growth names in the large-cap universe (but sometimes buys smaller firms or deep-value stocks).
If it weren't for David Williams's steady, smart moves, this fund would have been dead in the water a long time ago. This is Williams's baby through and through, and we think his presence is vital to the continued success of the fund.

When managers matter

Of course, not every manager change leads to a performance falloff. When legendary value investor Michael Price left Mutual Discovery in late 1998, many investors might have worried that the highly rated fund would come up short under new management. So far, though, things have gone investors' way. Despite a rough couple of years in 1999 and 2003, the fund has generally trounced other funds in its category since Price's departure.

Where Managers Matter Most—And Least

If you're looking for new investments and find two equally good funds, choose the one with the more experienced manager. But if the manager of a fund you already own jumps ship, it's not always best to sell the fund immediately.

Don't believe the hype

Occasionally, changes in management get a lot of media attention and investors get panicked. It's tempting to jump ship—especially if you can follow a manager you admire to a new fund. But don't move too fast. Management changes won't make a huge difference if your fund:

1 Is an index fund.
2 Is run by a team.
3 Is a fund from a strong family with deep analyst resources.
4 Is a steady performer.

Check out your fund's asset class (is it a modest bond fund?) and its historical volatility and performance range. Funds whose returns have varied little from year to year aren't likely to suffer unduly with a new manager at the helm. Moving in and out of funds costs money, so you're usually better off giving new management a chance to prove itself.

First, you may have to pay taxes on your sold shares, if they gained in value, and what you give up in taxes may not be offset by extra future gains in a different fund. Second, the new manager may do just as well as the old. Finally, some types of funds are simply less affected by manager changes than others. Here are some examples:

Index Funds. Managers of index funds are not actively choosing stocks, but simply mimicking a benchmark by owning the same stocks in the same proportion. As such, manager changes at index funds are less important than manager changes at actively managed funds. So if Gus Sauter leaves Vanguard 500 Index, don't sell. Although Sauter has added incremental returns to the fund during his tenure—the fund has been the best-performing S&P 500 index fund over the long term—the fund won't become a complete dog if Sauter leaves.

Funds in Categories with Modest Return Ranges. Managing an ultrashort-bond fund is a game of basis points. (A basis point is one-one hundredth of a percentage point.) In other words, because ultrashort bonds don't offer much return potential, the difference in return between a great and an awful ultrashort-bond fund is a matter of one or two percentage points. So if your ultrashort-bond fund manager leaves, it's probably not a big deal.

Funds from Families with Strong Benches. When a fund manager leaves Fidelity, we don't get very upset. Why? Because Fidelity has many talented managers and analysts who can pick up the slack. Manager changes aren't quite as troubling if you're talking about a fund from a family, such as Fidelity, T. Rowe Price, and American, with a number of good funds and a strong farm team.

Funds Run by Teams. While this isn't always the case, you'll often find that funds run by teams are less affected by manager changes than funds run by only one person. But that's only true if the fund really was run in a team fashion, in which decisions were truly democratic.

Conversely, then, manager changes can be a crushing blow to other types of funds. Investors who disregard managers and manager tenures in the following types of mutual funds may find themselves much worse off than a disappointed sports fan.

▶ One-manager funds.

▶ Funds run by very active managers who've proved to be adept stock-pickers or traders.

▶ Good funds from families that aren't strong overall, or from fund families that lack other strong funds with a similar investment style.

▶ Funds in specialized categories such as small growth or emerging markets, in which the range of possible returns is very wide.

Fearless Facts

▶ Management styles differ across funds. You'll need to identify one that you can live with.

▶ Like accountability? There's the single-manager approach. The manager gets help from a team of analysts but gets credit for all performance—good and bad.

▶ Want to ensure as much consistency as possible? Management teams work together to choose stocks and share a single strategy. That means that when one person leaves, the fund doesn't necessarily get a facelift.

▶ Desire a mix of styles or approaches? Choose a fund with multiple managers, all of whom work separately from each other. This approach is particularly popular for investors who like funds of funds.

▶ Know when management matters. Don't spend hours researching the manager's record at your index funds. This manager is never going to choose stocks; he's paid to copy a benchmark, not leave a personal mark on the offering.

Quiz

Answers to this quiz can be found on page 208

1 Funds following the multiple-manager system:

a Use two or more people who work together to choose investments.

b Use two or more people who work independently of each other to choose investments.

c Use one lead manager and a group of traders and research analysts.

2 Which type of fund is least affected by manager changes?

a Index funds.

b Funds in categories in which the range of return is wide.

c Funds from families that lack depth.

3 Which type of fund is most affected by manager changes?

a Funds in categories with modest return ranges.

b Funds run by teams.

c One-manager funds.

4 If you're choosing between two equally good funds, *do not* choose the one:

a From a fund family that's strong overall.

b Run by a single manager who's the only star in the fund family.

c That clearly identifies the length of the manager's tenure.

5 When a manager leaves a fund you own, you should:

a Sell immediately.

b Hold on.

c It depends.

Worksheet

Are your funds managed by a single manager, management team, or a multiple-manager system? In your opinion, which type of fund would be least affected by a manager change? Which would be affected the most?

Which management approach do you prefer? Why?

What do you think is the minimum amount of experience a fund manager should have? Do all of the funds that you own clear that hurdle?

Look across the funds in your portfolio. Do you own any funds run by "star managers"? Would you be inclined to sell when that manager retired or left for another firm, or hang on?

Lesson 111: Your First Fund

Throughout this book, you've learned how to evaluate funds so that you can answer five key questions: how has it performed, how risky has it been, what's in its portfolio, who's in charge, and how much does it cost. Those are questions you need to be able to answer whether you're choosing your first or your thirty-first fund. (Yes, some people own that many.)

When selecting your first stock fund, though, you need to focus on a few additional, specific things. Why? Because for some of you, your first fund may be your only fund—or your only fund for a while.

Here are the qualities to look for in your first fund.

Seek Diversification

Whether you're investing for a goal that's 5 or 50 years away, your first stock fund should be well diversified. That means the fund should hold a large number of stocks (100 or more) from a wide range of industries, or sectors. By looking at Morningstar's Fund Reports on Morningstar.com, you can find how many stocks a fund owns as well as which sectors it favors.

What's the big deal about diversification? Funds that own many stocks from many different sectors are generally more stable than funds holding few stocks from only one or two industries. For example, the average technology fund carried a standard deviation (a measure of volatility) of 43.4 in September 2002, while the average large-blend fund's standard deviation was a relatively sedate 17.1.

While you may own some of these more concentrated types of funds at some point in your investment life—say, to rev up your returns or to add some variety to your investments—they aren't suitable first-time investments. (We'll talk more about diversification and when you might focus on concentrated investments in later lessons.)

The first time you buy...	Buying your first mutual fund can be as nerve-wracking as buying a new car; it may not cost as much money, but if all goes well, it should be an even longer-lasting commitment! Most people need some help. Most people buying a car would do some comparison shopping and would check out available consumer reports, right? We want you to do the same. The mutual fund equivalents of *Consumer Reports* are everywhere, from magazines like *Money* and financial Web sites like Yahoo Finance and Morningstar.com to special mutual fund sections in some of the national newspapers. Many fund Web sites provide great introductions to the world of mutual funds too.

Favor Large Companies

Next, focus on funds that buy stocks of large U.S. companies. Funds with a collection of stocks such as Coca-Cola, Gillette, and Wal-Mart may not always offer the most exciting returns, but they tend to hold up better than smaller companies when times get tough.

Morningstar groups these funds, which are called large-cap funds, into three categories: large value, large blend, and large growth. Large-value funds own stocks that are undervalued, large-growth funds buy stocks that have strong growth prospects, and large-blend funds own a combination of the two.

Which should you choose? Large-growth funds are the most volatile of the three categories because they tend to own stocks in higher-growth, and therefore higher-risk, sectors, such as health care and technology. Large-value funds are generally less volatile but tend to perform in fits and starts, too, as they have their own pet sectors, such as financials and industrials. When these sectors do well, so will most large-value funds.

Your best choice would be a large-blend fund that owns both types of stocks. It has exposure to all of the aforementioned sectors.

Go with a Big Family

When buying your first fund, start with one of the larger fund families. Why? Giants such as Fidelity, Vanguard, and T. Rowe Price are closely monitored by the media and by investors. Intense public scrutiny has made it difficult for these shops to field really poor players for too long and while it's unlikely their funds will top the charts year in and year out, they're generally reliable.

Going with one of the bigger families has another benefit: Your first fund may not be your last fund, and the big families boast a range of offerings, from domestic large- and small-company funds to international options; taxable and tax-free bond offerings to single-sector funds. It's possible to build an entire portfolio from just one family.

But don't confuse big with diversified. Janus Funds, for example, is one of the industry's 10-largest families. While the group does offer international and bond funds, it's generally a large-growth specialist. You won't find much variety there.

To see how much variety a family offers, type in the name of the family in our Quotes/Reports box on Morningstar.com's home page. You'll find a list of Fund Reports for the family's funds. Go through some of the reports to get an idea of the types of funds the group offers or visit the fund family's Web site.

Diversification and Performance at a Glance

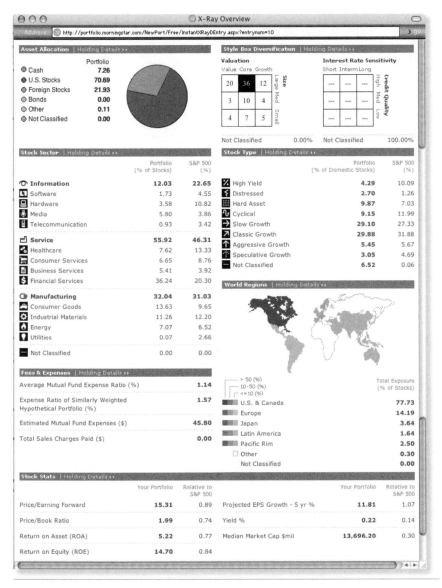

X-Ray Overview

Address: http://portfolio.morningstar.com/NewPort/Free/InstantXRayDEntry.aspx?entrynum=10

Asset Allocation | Holding Details ▸▸

	Portfolio
○ Cash	7.26
○ U.S. Stocks	70.69
○ Foreign Stocks	21.93
○ Bonds	0.00
○ Other	0.11
○ Not Classified	0.00

Style Box Diversification | Holding Details ▸▸

Valuation — Value Core Growth

20	36	12
3	10	4
4	7	5

Size: Large / Med / Small

Interest Rate Sensitivity — Short Interm Long

Credit Quality: High / Med / Low

Not Classified   0.00%   Not Classified   100.00%

Stock Sector | Holding Details ▸▸

	Portfolio (% of Stocks)	S&P 500 (%)
↻ **Information**	12.03	22.65
Software	1.73	4.55
Hardware	3.58	10.82
Media	5.80	3.86
Telecommunication	0.93	3.42
⊣ **Service**	55.92	46.31
Healthcare	7.62	13.33
Consumer Services	6.65	8.76
Business Services	5.41	3.92
Financial Services	36.24	20.30
⊡ **Manufacturing**	32.04	31.03
Consumer Goods	13.63	9.65
Industrial Materials	11.26	12.20
Energy	7.07	6.52
Utilities	0.07	2.66
▬ Not Classified	0.00	0.00

Stock Type | Holding Details ▸▸

	Portfolio (% of Domestic Stocks)	S&P 500 (%)
High Yield	4.29	10.09
Distressed	2.70	1.26
Hard Asset	9.87	7.03
Cyclical	9.15	11.99
Slow Growth	29.10	27.33
Classic Growth	29.88	31.88
Aggressive Growth	5.45	5.67
Speculative Growth	3.05	4.69
Not Classified	6.52	0.06

World Regions | Holding Details ▸▸

> 50 (%)
10-50 (%)
<= 10 (%)

	Total Exposure (% of Stocks)
U.S. & Canada	77.73
Europe	14.19
Japan	3.64
Latin America	1.64
Pacific Rim	2.50
☐ Other	0.30
Not Classified	0.00

Fees & Expenses | Holding Details ▸▸

Average Mutual Fund Expense Ratio (%)	1.14
Expense Ratio of Similarly Weighted Hypothetical Portfolio (%)	1.57
Estimated Mutual Fund Expenses ($)	45.80
Total Sales Charges Paid ($)	0.00

Stock Stats | Holding Details ▸▸

	Your Portfolio	Relative to S&P 500		Your Portfolio	Relative to S&P 500
Price/Earning Forward	15.31	0.89	Projected EPS Growth - 5 yr %	11.81	1.07
Price/Book Ratio	1.99	0.74	Yield %	0.22	0.14
Return on Asset (ROA)	5.22	0.77	Median Market Cap $mil	13,696.20	0.30
Return on Equity (ROE)	14.70	0.84			

Morningstar.com's Instant X-Ray tool provides you with a quick overview analysis of your portfolio. You'll get insight into your portfolio diversification and what is driving your portfolio's performance.

Fearless Facts

▶ **Your first fund should have it all...**
Demand diversification in your first fund—no matter what. It's far better to go with a moderate index offering that gives you exposure to a broad range of sectors, industries, and companies, than to chase after the latest hot fund with a focused portfolio.

▶ **Bigger really is better—the first time.**
If you're only going to buy one fund, there's no point in starting small. Your first fund should be an offering that plays in the large-cap arena. Why? Larger companies aren't immune to losses, but they do tend to be less volatile than their micro-cap rivals. After all, many small companies are just starting out and their prospects are uncertain.

▶ **Speaking from experience...**
Many die-hard investors choose index funds when it comes time for them to enter the investing arena. A good, cheap index offering—such as those fielded by the Vanguard family of funds—can offer broad exposure to a range of companies. Further, many of these funds sport low expense ratios and no loads. That means that down the road, you can change your mind without fear of huge penalties.

Quiz

1   Which would make the best first fund?

> a   One that owns 20 technology stocks.
>
> b   One that owns 100 financial stocks.
>
> c   One that owns 100 stocks from various sectors.

Answers to this quiz can be found on page 209

2   Why should your first fund be one that favors large companies?

> a   Because these funds are always the highest returning.
>
> b   Because these funds tend to be less volatile than funds owning smaller companies.
>
> c   Because these funds are cheap.

3   Which type of large-company fund generally makes the best first fund?

> a   Large value.
>
> b   Large blend.
>
> c   Large growth.

4   Why is it a bad idea to buy a single-sector fund as your first fund?

> a   Such funds are volatile.
>
> b   Such funds are poor performers.
>
> c   Such funds are expensive.

5   Which is not a reason for buying your first fund through one of the big fund families?

> a   Because their funds tend to be reliable.
>
> b   Because of the variety that big families usually offer.
>
> c   Because their funds are always the best performers.

Worksheet

Try to remember the first mutual fund you bought. What drew you to invest in that fund over others? Do you still own shares in that fund? Was your initial decision a good one?

If you are about to invest in your first mutual fund, why is diversification so important? Why are large-cap funds more appealing than small-cap funds for the core of your portfolio?

What do large fund families have to offer that appeals to first-time fund investors?

What are the possible drawbacks of investing with a very large fund family?

Lesson 112: What to Look For

Let's be honest: Very few investors are as geeky as Morningstar mutual fund analysts. Most people don't have time to fly around the country attending investment conferences and they don't waste their time swapping fund industry gossip. Furthermore, most investors have better things to do than to monitor dozens of funds. Finally, people starting out in investing probably don't have the money to buy more than one fund anyway.

So here's our advice for those searching for their first—and perhaps only—mutual fund.

Index Funds

Index funds are about as simple as it gets. You might remember from **Lesson 110: Why Knowing Your Fund Manager Matters** that index-fund managers aren't picking stocks in the traditional sense. Instead, they are buying the same stocks in the same proportion as they appear in a particular index. In other words, they don't buy a stock because they like a company's prospects or sell because a firm's outlook has become less than rosy. They simply own the index. They are passive investors.

Index funds have plenty of benefits. Most important, they tend to be low in cost. For example, Vanguard 500 Index's expense ratio is just 0.18% versus 1.02% for the typical large-blend fund. Because the index-fund managers aren't actively managing their funds—instead of making buy and sell decisions, they're simply doing what the index does—management fees tend to be low.

Index funds are also advantageous because they are fairly predictable. First, they tend to return what the index does, minus their expenses. Second, they always own what the index owns, which means they tend to be style-specific. For example, if a fund indexes the S&P 500, that means it owns large-blend stocks; it'll own those types of stocks today, tomorrow, and the next day. You know what to expect from an index fund. Funds that aren't indexed, also called actively managed funds, might not own the same types of stocks day in and day out. It all depends on the manager's style. He or she may like large companies one day and then see value in smaller firms the next.

Finally, index-fund investors don't have to worry about manager turnover: If the manager leaves, the next manager is likely to do just as well, as long as the mutual fund shop's resources haven't changed. Nor is asset size an issue. Index funds can handle plenty of assets because they generally don't use fast-trading strategies.

If you only plan to own one index fund for a while, make sure it favors large companies. Some funds, including Vanguard Total Stock Market Index, hold stocks of all sizes, though larger companies are most heavily represented. Such funds would be excellent choices for one-fund owners.

Funds of Funds

Funds of funds are mutual funds that invest in other mutual funds. That may sound redundant, but it's true.

Just as a regular mutual fund offers the skills of a professional manager who assembles a portfolio of stocks or other securities, the manager of a fund of funds will select a portfolio of funds, managed by other managers.

If you have only a small amount to invest each month, a fund of funds allows you access to more funds than you might be able to afford on your own. It also allows investors to avoid the recordkeeping and paperwork that comes with owning an assortment of funds. So what's the catch? Expenses, mostly. The fund of funds structure creates a double layer of costs. First, there are the expenses associated with running the fund of funds itself—management fees, administrative costs, etc. Second, there are the costs associated with the underlying funds—the same sorts of management fees, administrative costs, and so on. A fund of funds may report an expense ratio of just 1%, but keep in mind that you're still paying the expense ratios on each and every fund that the fund of funds owns.

Some fine funds of funds eliminate the double-fee problem. Families such as T. Rowe Price and Vanguard offer funds of funds that invest only in their own funds. The families then waive the cost of the funds of funds—their reported expense ratios are 0%—and you only pay the costs of the underlying funds. Obviously, these funds are a much cheaper option.

Life-cycle Funds

First introduced in the early 1990s, life-cycle funds offer investors premixed doses of stocks, bonds, and cash according to their age and risk tolerance. Most fund families offer life-cycle funds in three formulas—aggressive, moderate, and conservative—that you can cycle through as you progress from a young, aggressive investor to an older, more conservative one. Some life-cycle funds are funds of funds, while others own individual securities outright.

All the life-cycle series share the same goal of first growing and then preserving your portfolio, but they vary in their methods. Some track indexes and maintain a more or less static mix of assets. Most life-cycle offerings, however, invest more actively. Even Vanguard, which promotes a passive indexing strategy in its LifeStrategy brochure, invests 25% of each life-cycle portfolio in the actively managed Vanguard Asset Allocation.

In the hands of the right manager, such active management can produce good results. But when an active manager concentrates in an asset class at the wrong time, tactical shifts can be deadly. If such maneuvers make you nervous, then a passive index approach might suit you better.

Use one of our most straightforward tools—Morningstar's Premium Fund Screener, available to all Premium members of Morningstar.com—to search for funds that are:

Screening for funds

1 Diversified. Using the Screener tool, choose "Equity Style = Blend."
2 Large cap. Using the tool, next choose "Equity Style = Large Blend."
3 From a large family. Using the tool, next choose "Name = [some large fund family name]." Some of our favorites include Vanguard, T. Rowe Price, American Century, and Fidelity.

Fearless Facts

▶ Look for a fund that holds more than 100 stocks and is diversified across industries. No focused funds. No sector funds. No kidding.

▶ If you can buy only one, buy big. Funds that invest in large companies have generally been less volatile than those that focus on the tiny players.

▶ Go with a name brand. Senior fund shops are senior for a reason—they haven't gone out of business. Explore the options at the respected old-school firms, such as Vanguard and T. Rowe Price. After all, they've endured plenty of media scrutiny, and there's a lot of public information available about their funds.

▶ Give yourself a break. Consider an index fund, a life-cycle fund, or a fund of funds.

At an index fund, you won't have to worry about manager changes, quick turnover rates, or asset size. Meanwhile, a life-cycle fund is tailored (or at least semi-tailored) to your needs (well, the needs of a hypothetical person who sort of matches your profile). Finally, a fund of funds often provides diversification, access to different investment styles, and a broad array of equity and bond choices.

Quiz

1   An index-fund manager:

   a   Buys stocks that he likes.

   b   Buys what an index does.

   c   Sells stocks when he doesn't like them.

Answers to this quiz can be found on page 210

2   Which is not an advantage of indexing?

   a   Low costs.

   b   Predictability.

   c   Great stock-picking.

3   Funds of funds directly buy:

   a   Stocks.

   b   Bonds.

   c   Other mutual funds.

4   The main drawback to most funds of funds is:

   a   Hidden costs.

   b   Extra paperwork.

   c   High up-front investment minimums.

5   Life-cycle funds:

   a   Are all index funds.

   b   Invest to fit an investor's age and risk tolerance.

   c   Are all actively managed.

Worksheet

Look at the funds in your portfolio or 401(k) plan. Would you say you have devoted an adequate percentage to so-called "core" funds?

Why are index funds a good investment choice for first-time investors?

What do funds of funds have to offer, especially to first-time investors? What do you have to watch out for when looking at funds of funds?

Why are life-cycle funds a good long-term option? What are their risks?

continued...

Between index funds, funds of funds, and life-cycle funds, which do you think is the best fit for your first investment? Which minimizes risk? Which has the lowest expenses? How should these factors play into your investment decision?

Investing Terms

A

Alpha

A measure of the difference between a fund's actual returns and its expected performance, given its level of risk as measured by beta. A positive alpha figure indicates the fund has performed better than its beta would predict. In contrast, a negative alpha indicates the fund's underperformance, given the expectations established by the fund's beta. Alpha depends on two factors: the assumption that market risk, as measured by beta, is the only risk measure necessary, and the strength of the linear relationship between the fund and the index, as it has been measured by R-squared.

Annual Returns

Morningstar calculates annual total returns on a calendar-year and year-to-date basis. The year-to-date return is updated daily on Morningstar.com. For mutual funds, return includes both income (in the form of dividends or interest payments) and capital gains or losses (the increase or decrease in the value of a security). Morningstar calculates total return by taking the change in a fund's NAV, assuming the reinvestment of all income and capital-gains distributions (on the actual reinvestment date used by the fund) during the period, and then dividing by the initial NAV. Unless total returns are marked as load-adjusted, Morningstar does not adjust total return for sales charges or for redemption fees. Total returns do account for management, administrative, and 12b-1 fees and other costs automatically deducted from fund assets.

Automatic-Investment Plan

An arrangement by which investors may initiate an account with a fund with a very small investment up front, with the condition that they agree to invest a fixed amount per month in the future.

Average Credit Quality/Credit Quality

In Morningstar.com products, average credit quality gives a snapshot of the portfolio's overall credit quality. It is an average of each bond's credit rating, adjusted for its relative weighting in the portfolio. For corporate-bond and municipal-bond funds, Morningstar also shows the percentage of fixed-income securities that fall within each credit-quality rating, as assigned by Standard & Poor's or Moody's. U.S. government bonds carry the highest credit rating, while bonds issued by speculative or bankrupt companies usually carry the lowest credit ratings. Anything at or below BB is considered a high-yield or "junk" bond.

Average Weighted Price

Morningstar generates this figure from the fund's portfolio by weighting the price of each bond by its relative size in the portfolio. This number reveals if the fund favors bonds selling at prices above or below face value (premium or discount securities, respectively). A higher number indicates a bias toward premiums. This statistic is expressed as a percentage of par (face) value. Average weighted price can reflect current market expectations. Morningstar generates this figure from the fund's portfolio, by weighting the price of each bond by its relative size in the portfolio.

B

Bear Market

A period when investment values drop. Bear markets can exist for certain kinds of investments (such as small-company stocks), for an index (such as the S&P 500), or marketwide. Bear markets usually aren't labeled as such until values have slipped by 20%. Its opposite is called a bull market.

Bear Market % Rank

In Morningstar products, the bear-market percentile rank details how a fund has performed during bear markets. For stock funds, a bear market is defined as all months in the past five years that the S&P 500 lost more than 3%; for bond funds, it's all months in the past five years that the Lehman Brothers Aggregate Bond Index lost more than 1%. Morningstar adds a fund's performance during each bear-market month to arrive at a total bear-market return. Based on these returns, each fund is then assigned a percentile ranking. Stock funds are ranked separately from bond funds. Use this figure to analyze how well a fund performs during market downturns, relative to its peers.

Benchmark

What you compare your fund's returns with to judge its performance. A benchmark can be the average performance of funds similar to yours or a broad index of the investments your fund usually picks from. The S&P 500 Index is a good benchmark for funds that buy large-company stocks, for example.

Best Fit Alpha

In Morningstar products, this is the alpha of the fund relative to its Best Fit Index. Alpha is a measure of the difference between a fund's actual returns and its expected performance given its level of risk as measured by beta. A positive alpha figure indicates the fund has performed better than its beta would predict. In contrast, a negative alpha indicates the fund has underperformed given the expectations established by its beta.

Best Fit Beta

On Morningstar.com, this is the beta of the fund relative to its Best Fit Index. Beta is a measure of a fund's sensitivity to market movements. The beta of the market is 1.00 by definition. Morningstar calculates beta by comparing a fund's excess return over Treasury bills to the Best Fit Index's excess return over Treasury bills. A beta of 1.10 shows that the fund has performed 10% better than its Best Fit Index in up markets and 10% worse in down markets, assuming all other factors remained constant.

Best Fit Index

Morningstar defines this as the market index that shows the highest correlation with a fund over the most recent 36 months, as measured by the highest R-squared. Morningstar regresses a fund's monthly excess returns against the monthly excess returns of several well-known market indexes. Both the standard and best-fit results can be useful to investors. The standard index R-squared statistics can help investors plan the diversification of their portfolio of funds. For example, an investor who wishes to diversify and already owns a fund with a very high correlation (and thus high R-squared) with the S&P 500 might choose not to buy another fund that correlates closely to that index. In addition, the best-fit index can be used to compare the betas and alphas of similar funds that show the same best-fit index. Morningstar recalculates the best-fit index in-house on a monthly basis.

Beta

A measure of a fund's sensitivity to market movements. The beta of the market is 1.00 by definition. Morningstar calculates beta by comparing a fund's excess return over Treasury bills to the market's excess return over Treasury bills, so a beta of 1.10 shows that the fund has performed 10% better than its benchmark index in up markets and 10% worse in down markets, assuming all other factors remain constant. Conversely, a beta of 0.85 indicates that the fund is expected to perform 15% worse than the market during up markets and 15% better during down markets. Beta can be a useful tool when at least some of a fund's performance history can be explained by the market as a whole. Beta is particularly appropriate when used to measure the risk of a combined portfolio of mutual funds. It is important to note that a low beta for a fund does not necessarily imply that the fund has a low level of volatility. A low beta signifies only that the fund's market-related risk is low.

Bond

A loan you make to a company or government for a certain time (the bond's term or maturity) typically in return for regular interest payments (the bond's coupon). Interest from some government bonds, particularly municipal bonds, may be tax-free.

Broker

The "intermediary" between you and the other investors, a broker buys and sells securities for you for a fee, called a commission. There are many kinds of brokers, from online brokers, who allow you to trade cheaply over the Internet, to full-service brokers, who provide advice and other services.

Bull Market

A good time for investors! Stock prices rise during a bull market. And when stock prices go up, investors (usually) make money. Investors who think the stock market will continue to go up are called bulls. The opposite of a bull market is called a bear market.

C

Capital Appreciation

A gain in the value of a stock or bond. The amount of appreciation is measured by subtracting the purchase price from the current price.

Capital Gain/Loss

The difference between what you pay for a stock or other investment and what you sell it for. In other words, your profit or loss. If you buy shares of Great Company for $100 and sell them for $250, your capital gain is $150. You pay taxes on capital gains.

Cash Flow

Basically, what a company makes minus what it spends. A company's cash flow is its income (minus investment earnings) less what it spends on rent, equipment, and other costs. Some investors use cash flow instead of earnings to judge how well a company is doing.

Closed-End Funds

An investment that acts like a cross between a mutual fund and a stock. Like a mutual fund, it invests a pool of money in a variety of investments. Like a stock, however, it issues a limited number of shares that can trade at prices different from the value of its investments.

Closed Fund

An open-end fund that has closed, either temporarily or permanently, to new investors. This usually occurs when management finds the fund's increasing asset size to be disadvantageous.

Closed to All Investments

Funds that are accepting no investments whatsoever, even from current shareholders.

Closed to New Investments

If funds are closed to new investments, they are not accepting new shareholder investments. This does not, however, restrict current shareholders from increasing their investment amount.

Commission

What you pay a broker or financial advisor to buy or sell investments for you. Commissions can be a percentage of your trade (for example, 5% of a $10,000 trade equals a $500 commission) or a set fee. You usually pay a higher commission the more services your broker provides.

Composition

The composition percentages on Morningstar.com provide a simple breakdown of a fund's portfolio holdings, as of the date listed, into general investment classes. Cash encompasses both the actual cash and the cash equivalents (fixed-income securities with maturities of one year or less) held by the portfolio. Negative percentages of cash indicate that the portfolio is leveraged, meaning it has borrowed against its own assets to buy more securities or that it has used other techniques to gain additional exposure to the market.

Compounding

When your interest earns interest. If you invest $10,000 and generate a return of 10%, you'll have $11,000 at the end of the year. If you earn 10% again the next year, both your initial investment and your $1,000 in interest earn interest, for a new total of $12,100. Over time, compounding's effect is powerful.

Coupon

The fixed percentage paid out on a fixed-income security on an annual basis.

Credit Analysis

For corporate-bond and municipal-bond funds, the credit analysis depicts the quality of bonds in the fund's portfolio. The analysis reveals the percentage of fixed-income securities that fall within each credit-quality rating as assigned by Standard & Poor's or Moody's. At the top of the ratings are U.S. government bonds. Bonds issued and backed by the federal government are of extremely high quality and thus are considered superior to bonds rated AAA, which is the highest possible rating a corporate issue can receive. Morningstar gives U.S. government bonds a credit rating separate from AAA securities to allow for a more accurate credit analysis of a portfolio's holdings. Bonds with a BBB rating are the lowest bonds that are still considered to be of investment grade. Bonds that are rated BB or lower (often called junk bonds or high-yield bonds) are considered to be quite speculative. Like the style box, the credit analysis can help determine whether or not a fund's portfolio meets a desired standard or quality. It can also shed light on the management strategy of the fund. If the fund holds a large percentage of assets in lower-quality issues, for example, then the fund follows a more aggressive style and is probably more concerned with yield than credit quality.

Credit Risk

The chance that you won't be able to get interest payments or your money back from the issuer that sold you a bond. Government bonds have low credit risk, while junk bonds from companies with shaky credit have high credit risk.

D

Developed Markets

Morningstar characterizes the following as developed markets: Australia, Austria, Belgium, Canada, Denmark, Finland, France, Germany, Ireland, Italy, Japan, Luxembourg, the Netherlands, New Zealand, Norway, Singapore, Spain, Sweden, Switzerland, the United Kingdom, the United States, and a handful of smaller countries and territories (such as Gibraltar). All other countries are considered emerging markets. Emerging markets normally carry greater political and economic risk than developed countries, and stocks located in them are normally less liquid and more volatile.

Diversification

Spreading your money over many different investments. When you're diversified, if one investment does badly for a while, you may still make money from your other investments. Diversification generally lowers risk.

Dividends

Money taken from a company's profits and paid to stockholders. Companies aren't required to pay dividends. Dividends are paid to you either in cash or in more stock. Mutual funds that own dividend-paying stock must pass the dividends along to their shareholders each year.

Dollar-Cost Averaging

A way to buy more of an investment when it's cheaper and less when it's expensive. To dollar-cost average, you simply invest the same amount of money every week, month, or paycheck so that, as an investment's price falls, you automatically buy more shares.

Duration

One measure of the interest-rate sensitivity of a bond or bond fund. Bond funds with long durations will do well when interest rates are declining but suffer as interest rates rise. Short-duration bond funds are less volatile but offer fewer potential gains.

E

Earnings-per-Share Growth %

This figure for Morningstar products represents the annualized rate of net-income-per-share growth over the trailing one-year period for the stocks held by a fund. Earnings-per-share growth gives a good picture of the rate at which a company has grown its profitability per unit of equity. All things being equal, stocks with higher earnings-per-share growth rates are generally more desirable than those with slower earnings-per-share growth rates. One of the important differences between earnings-per-share growth rates and net-income growth rates is that the former reflects the dilution that occurs from new stock issuance, the exercise of employee stock options, warrants, convertible securities, and share repurchases.

Emerging Markets

Morningstar characterizes the following as developed markets: Australia, Austria, Belgium, Canada, Denmark, Finland, France, Germany, Ireland, Italy, Japan, Luxembourg, the Netherlands, New Zealand, Norway, Singapore, Spain, Sweden, Switzerland, the United Kingdom, the United States, and a handful of smaller countries and territories (such as Gibraltar). All other countries are considered emerging markets. Emerging markets normally carry greater political and economic risk than developed countries, and stocks located in them are normally less liquid and more volatile.

Enhanced-Index Funds

Like index funds, this group includes funds that attempt to match an index's performance. Unlike an index fund, however, enhanced-index funds typically attempt to better the index by adding value or reducing volatility through selective stock-picking.

Exchange-Traded Funds

At the most basic level, exchange-traded funds are just what their name implies: baskets of securities that are traded, like individual stocks, on an exchange. Unlike regular open-end mutual funds, ETFs are priced throughout the trading day. They can also be sold short and bought on margin—anything you might do with a stock, you can do with an ETF. They often also charge lower annual expenses than even the least costly index mutual funds. However, as with stocks, you must pay a commission to buy and sell ETF shares, which can be a significant drawback for those who trade frequently or invest regular sums of money.

Expense Ratio

The annual expense ratio, taken from the fund's annual report, expresses the percentage of assets deducted each fiscal year for fund expenses, including 12b-1 fees, management fees, administrative fees, operating costs, and all other asset-based costs incurred by the fund. Portfolio transaction fees, or brokerage costs, as well as initial or deferred sales charges are not included in the expense ratio. The expense ratio, which is deducted from the fund's average net assets, is accrued on a daily basis. Funds may also opt to waive all or a portion of the expenses that make up their overall expense ratio. The expense ratio is useful because it shows the actual amount that a fund takes out of its assets each year to cover its expenses. Investors should note not only the current expense-ratio figure, but also the trend in these expenses; it could prove useful to know whether a fund is becoming cheaper or more costly. Overall, expenses can have a meaningful impact on long-term results, so investors should try to invest in funds with below-average expenses.

F

Fees and Expenses

Morningstar distinguishes among the myriad fees and expenses encountered with mutual funds. The different expenses and their characteristics are listed as follows.

Administrative Costs—What your fund charges you in order to pay for its day-to-day operations, including renting office space, printing prospectuses, and keeping records. You'll never write a check for this fee, though, because administrative costs, like the other parts of your fund's expense ratio, are deducted directly from your fund's returns.

Deferred Load—Also called a contingent deferred sales charge or back-end load, a deferred load is an alternative to the traditional front-end sales charge, as it is deducted only at the time of sale of fund shares. The deferred-load structure commonly decreases to zero over a period of time. A typical deferred load's structure might have a 5% charge if shares are redeemed within the first year of ownership and decline by a percentage point each year thereafter. These loads are normally applied to the lesser of original share price or current market value. It is important to note that although the deferred load declines each year, the accumulated annual distribution and services charges (the total 12b-1 fee) usually offset this decline.

Front-End Load—The initial sales charge or front-end load is a deduction made from each investment in the fund. The amount is generally based on the amount of the investment. Larger investments, both initial and cumulative, generally receive percentage discounts based on the dollar value invested. A typical front-end load might have a 4.75% charge for purchases less than $50,000, which decreases as the amount of the investment increases. Investors who have significant assets and work with a financial advisor are therefore better off buying front-load shares than deferred-load shares.

Management Fee—The management fee is the maximum percentage deducted from a fund's average net assets to pay an advisor or subadvisor. Often, as the fund's net assets grow, the percentage deducted for management fees decreases. Alternatively, the fund may compute the fee as a flat percentage of average net assets. A portion of the management fee may also be charged in the form of a group fee. To determine the group fee, the fund family creates a sliding scale for the family's total net assets and determines a percentage applied to each fund's asset base. The management fee might also be amended by or be primarily composed of a performance fee, which raises or lowers the management fee based on the fund's returns relative to an established index.

No-Load—These funds charge no sales or 12b-1 fees.

Redemption Fee—The redemption fee is an amount charged when money is withdrawn from the fund before a predetermined period elapses. This fee usually does not go back into the pockets of the fund company, but rather into the fund itself and thus does not represent a net cost to shareholders. Also, unlike contingent-deferred sales charges, redemption fees typically operate only in short, specific time clauses, commonly 30, 180, or 365 days. However, some redemption fees exist for up to five years. Charges are not imposed after the stated time has passed. These fees are typically imposed to discourage market-timers, whose quick movements into and out of funds can be disruptive. The charge is normally imposed on the ending share value, appreciated or depreciated from the original value.

Service Fee—The service fee is part of the total 12b-1 fee. Capped at a maximum 0.25%, the service fee is designed to compensate financial planners or brokers for ongoing shareholder-liaison services, which may include responding to customer inquiries and providing information on investments. An integral component of level-load and deferred-load funds, the fees were previously known as a trail commission. Only service fees adopted pursuant to Rule 12b-1 are tracked. Despite the implication of its name, service fees do not act as compensation for transfer agency or custodial services.

12b-1—The 12b-1 fee represents the maximum annual charge deducted from fund assets to pay for distribution and marketing costs. This fee is expressed as a percentage. Some funds may be permitted to impose 12b-1 fees but are currently waiving all or a portion of the fees. Total allowable 12b-1 fees, excluding loads, are capped at 1% of average net assets annually. Of this, the distribution and marketing portion of the fee may account for up to 0.75%. The other portion of the overall 12b-1 fee, the service fee, is listed separately and may account for up to 0.25%. Often, funds charging a 12b-1 fee will allow shareholders to convert into a share class without the fee after a certain number of years. (These are normally deferred-load funds.)

Fixed Income

An investment that pays a specific interest rate, such as a bond, a certificate of deposit, or preferred stock. Mutual funds composed of fixed-income instruments (like bond funds) typically pay a variable rate of interest.

401(k) Plan

An employer-sponsored retirement plan. It lets you invest part of your paycheck—before taxes are deducted—in investments, such as mutual funds, that you choose from the plan. Your 401(k) money isn't taxed until you start withdrawing it, usually at retirement.

Fund Advisor

This is the company or companies that are given primary responsibility for managing a fund's portfolio.

Fund Family

A fund family is a company that offers mutual funds. Generally speaking, the company name is included in the official fund name.

Fund Inception Date

The date on which the fund began its operations. Funds with long track records offer more history by which investors can assess overall fund performance. However, another important factor to consider is the fund manager and his or her tenure with the fund. Often a change in fund performance can indicate a change in management.

Fund of Funds

A mutual fund that invests in other mutual funds. The goal is to give you maximum diversification with a single investment. You might think of it as buying an assortment of chocolates in a box, rather than separately. One difference: With a fund of funds, you often pay extra for the "box."

G

Growth Measures

Book-Value Growth—Book value is, in theory, what would be left over for shareholders if a company shut down its operations, paid off all its creditors, collected from all its debtors, and liquidated itself. In practice, however, the value of assets and liabilities can change substantially from when they are first recorded. Book-value growth shows the rate of increase in a company's book value per share, based on up to four periodic time periods. When reported for a mutual fund, it shows the weighted average of the growth rates in book value for each stock in the fund's portfolio. This measure helps determine Morningstar's growth score for each stock and the overall growth orientation of the fund.

Cash-Flow Growth—Cash flow tells you how much cash a business is actually generating from its earnings before depreciation, amortization, and non-cash charges. Sometimes called cash earnings, it's considered a gauge of liquidity and solvency. Cash-flow growth shows the rate of increase in a company's cash flow per share, based on up to four time periods. When reported for a mutual fund, it shows the weighted average of the growth in cash flow for each stock in the fund's portfolio. This measure helps determine Morningstar's growth score for each stock and the overall growth orientation of the fund.

Growth of $10,000 Graph—The Growth of $10,000 graph shows a fund's performance based on how $10,000 invested in a fund would have grown over time. The returns used in the graph are not load-adjusted. The growth of $10,000 begins at the date of the fund's inception, or the first year listed on the graph, whichever is appropriate.

Historical Earnings Growth—Historical earnings growth shows the rate of increase in a company's earnings per share, based on up to four periodic time periods. When reported for a mutual fund, it shows the weighted average of the growth in earnings for each stock in the fund's portfolio. This measure helps determine Morningstar's growth score for each stock and the overall growth orientation of the fund.

Long-Term Earnings Growth—Earnings are what is left of a firm's revenues after it pays all of its expenses, costs, and taxes. Companies whose earnings grow faster than those of their industry peers usually see better price performance for their stocks. Projected earnings growth is an estimate of a company's expected long-term growth in earnings, derived from all polled analysts' estimates. When reported for a mutual fund, it shows the weighted average of the projected growth in earnings for each stock in the fund's portfolio. This measure helps determine Morningstar's growth score for each stock and the overall growth orientation of the fund.

Sales Growth—Sales growth shows the rate of increase in a company's sales per share, based on up to four periodic time periods, and is considered the best gauge of how rapidly a company's core business is growing. When reported for a mutual fund, it shows the weighted average of the sales-growth rates for each stock in the fund's portfolio. This measure helps determine Morningstar's growth score for each stock and the overall growth orientation of the fund.

H

Hedge Fund

A hedge fund is like a mutual fund on steroids. Most hedge funds have really high minimum investments, often $1 million or more, and are allowed to make risky investments that mutual funds aren't. Hence, they can make and lose lots of money.

I

Index Funds

Funds that track a particular index and attempt to match its returns. While an index typically has a much larger portfolio than a mutual fund, the fund's management may study the index's movements to develop a representative sampling and match sectors proportionately.

Individual Retirement Account (IRA)

A tax-deferred retirement account that permits individuals to set aside tax-deferred earnings each year. IRAs can be established at a bank, mutual fund, or brokerage.

Institutional Funds

A mutual fund that generally only sells shares to big players such as pension plans. The typical institutional fund has a high minimum investment, typically $100,000 or more. You may be able to get into an institutional fund for less through online brokers or an employer retirement plan.

Interest-Rate Sensitivity

How much the value of a bond or bond fund changes when interest rates shift. Bond values move in the opposite direction from interest rates. Duration is one common measure of interest-rate sensitivity.

L

Life-cycle Funds

These funds are designed to be an investor's sole investment. Usually designated as aggressive, moderate, or conservative, these funds typically hold a mix of stocks and bonds.

Liquidity

A way to describe how easily you can sell an investment for cash. Your savings account, for instance, has lots of liquidity because you can get at your money anytime. Stocks that are traded a lot are also very liquid. Little-known stocks and most collectibles are considered illiquid.

M

Management Team

This applies to funds in which there are two or more people involved in fund management, and they manage together, or when the fund strongly promotes its team-managed aspect.

Manager Tenure

This represents the number of years that the current manager has been the portfolio manager of the fund. Fund management is clearly an important variable in fund performance. If you buy a fund for its long-term performance, for example, you'll want to be sure that the manager responsible for the good record is still at his or her post. Likewise, if an improvement in fund performance correlates with the arrival of a new manager, investors should downplay the fund's previous record and focus on the performance attributable to the new management.

Market Capitalization

For domestic-stock offerings, this measures the portfolio's "center of gravity," in terms of the size of companies in which it invests. A market capitalization is calculated for each stock. Its weight in the average weighted market-cap calculation is then determined by the percentage of stocks it consumes in the overall portfolio. For example, a stock that is a 10% position in a fund will have twice as much influence on the calculation than a stock that is a 5% stake.

Market-Neutral Funds

These are funds that attempt to eliminate the risks of the market, typically by holding 50% of assets in long positions in stocks and 50% of assets in short positions. Funds in this group match the characteristics of their long and short portfolios, keeping factors such as P/E ratios and industry exposure similar. Stock-picking, rather than broad market moves, should drive a market-neutral fund's performance.

Market Risk

The chance that an entire group of investments, such as U.S. stocks, will lose value (as opposed to one particular stock falling in price). Market risk is a danger because there's always the chance you'll have to sell an investment when the market is down.

Market-Timing

This is an investment strategy in which investors switch in and out of securities or between types of mutual funds in the hopes of benefiting from various economic and technical indicators that are thought to presage market moves.

Market Value

The current value of the security. For stocks, the market value is the security price times the number of shares held.

185

For bonds, the market value is the bond price multiplied by the number of bonds held.

Maturity

How long you must wait before a bond repays you. For instance, a 30-year bond pays you interest for 30 years, then repays you your investment, or principal. The longer the maturity, the riskier the bond, because you must wait longer before reinvesting your money.

Mean

Represents the annualized total return for a fund over 3-, 5-, and 10-year time periods.

Minimum Investments

Initial Investment—The minimum purchase indicates the smallest investment amount a fund will accept to establish a new account.

Additional Investment—This indicates the smallest additional purchase amount a fund will accept in an existing account.

Initial Auto-Invest Program Investment—This indicates the smallest amount with which one may enter a fund's automatic-investment plan—an arrangement in which the fund takes money on a monthly, quarterly, semi-annual, or annual basis from the shareholder's checking account. The systematic investment amount is the minimum amount required for subsequent regular investments in an automatic investment plan. Studies indicate that regular automatic investment, also known as dollar-cost averaging, is perhaps the most successful investment plan for long-term investors.

Additional Auto-Invest Program Investment—This indicates the smallest additional investment amount a fund will accept in an existing automatic-investment plan account.

Money Market—Similar to a savings account, only usually paying you a better interest rate. Money-market funds invest in extremely short-term instruments. As a result, they're ultrasafe and you can withdraw exactly what you've deposited at any time.

Morningstar Category

While the investment objective stated in a fund's prospectus may or may not reflect how the fund actually invests, a Morningstar category is assigned based on the underlying securities in each portfolio. Morningstar categories help investors and investment professionals make meaningful comparisons between funds. The categories make it easier to build well-diversified portfolios, assess potential risk, and identify top-performing funds. We place funds in a given category based on their portfolio statistics and compositions over the past three years. If the fund is new and has no portfolio history, we estimate where it will fall before giving it a more permanent category assignment. When necessary, we may change a category assignment based on recent changes to the portfolio.

Domestic-Stock Funds—Funds with at least 70% of assets in domestic stocks are categorized based on the style and size of the stocks they typically own. The style and size divisions reflect those used in the Morningstar style box: value, blend, or growth style and small, medium, or large median market capitalization.

International-Stock Funds—Stock funds that have invested 40% or more of their equity holdings in foreign stocks (on average over the past three years) are placed in one of the following international-stock categories:

Asia/Pacific ex-Japan—At least 75% of stocks invested in Pacific countries, with less than 10% of stocks invested in Japan.

Diversified Emerging Markets—At least 50% of stocks invested in emerging markets.

Diversified Pacific—At least 65% of stocks invested in Pacific countries, with at least an additional 10% of stocks invested in Japan.

Europe—At least 75% of stocks invested in Europe.

Foreign—An international fund having no more than 20% of stocks invested in the United States.

Japan—At least 75% of stocks invested in Japan.

Latin America—At least 75% of stocks invested in Latin America.

World—An international fund having more than 20% of stocks invested in the United States.

World Allocation—Used for funds with stock holdings of greater than 20% but less than 70% of the portfolio where 40% of the stocks and bonds are foreign.

Bond Funds—Funds with 80% or more of their assets invested in bonds are classified as bond funds. Bond funds are divided into two main groups: taxable bond and municipal bond. (Note: For all bond funds, maturity figures are used only when duration figures are unavailable.)

Municipal-Bond Funds
High-Yield Municipal—A fund that invests at least 50% of assets in high-income municipal securities that are not rated or that are rated by a major rating agency at the level of BBB (considered speculative in the municipal industry) or below.

Municipal National Long-Term—A national fund with an average duration of more than 7 years, or average maturity of more than 12 years.

Municipal National Intermediate-Term—A national fund with an average duration of more than 4.5 years but less than 7 years, or average maturity of more than 5 years but less than 12 years.

Municipal National Short—A fund that focuses on municipal bonds with an average duration of less than 4.5 years, or an average maturity of less than five years.

State-Specific Munis—A municipal-bond fund that primarily invests in one specific state. These funds must have at least 80% of assets invested in municipal bonds from that state. Each state-specific muni category includes long, intermediate, and short-duration bond funds.

Taxable-Bond Funds

Long-Term Government—A fund with at least 90% of bond portfolio invested in government issues with a duration of greater than or equal to 6 years, or an average effective maturity of greater than 10 years.

Intermediate-Term Government—A fund with at least 90% of its bond portfolio invested in government issues with a duration of greater than or equal to 3.5 years and less than six years, or an average effective maturity of greater than or

equal to four years and less than 10 years.

Short-Term Government—A fund with at least 90% of its bond portfolio invested in government issues with a duration of greater than or equal to one year and less than 3.5 years, or average effective maturity of greater than or equal to one year and less than four years.

Long-Term Bond—A fund that focuses on corporate and other investment-grade issues with an average duration of more than 6 years, or an average effective maturity of more than 10 years.

Intermediate-Term Bond—A fund that focuses on corporate, government, foreign, or other issues with an average duration of greater than or equal to 3.5 years but less than or equal to 6 years, or an average effective maturity of more than 4 years but less than 10 years.

Short-Term Bond—A fund that focuses on corporate and other investment-grade issues with an average duration of more than one year but less than 3.5 years, or an average effective maturity of more than one year but less than four years.

Ultrashort Bond—Used for funds with an average duration or an average effective maturity of less than one year. This category includes general- and government-bond funds, and excludes any international, convertible, multisector, and high-yield bond funds.

Bank Loan—A fund that invests primarily in floating-rate bank loans instead of bonds. In exchange for their credit risk, these funds offer high interest payments that typically float above a common short-term benchmark.

World Bond—A fund that invests at least 40% of bonds in foreign markets.

Emerging-Markets Bond—A fund that invests at least 65% of assets in emerging-markets bonds.

High-Yield Bond—A fund with at least 65% of assets in bonds rated below BBB.

Multisector Bond—Used for funds that seek income by diversifying their assets among several fixed-income sectors, usually U.S. government obligations, foreign bonds, and high-yield domestic debt securities.

Morningstar Rating for Funds

A measure of how well a mutual fund has balanced risk and return. We compare a fund's long-term risk-adjusted performance with that of its category peers. A 5-star rating is the best; 1 star is the worst.

Morningstar Risk

An assessment of the variations in a fund's monthly returns, with an emphasis on downside variations, in comparison to similar funds. In each Morningstar Category, the 10% of funds with the lowest measured risk are described as Low Risk, the next 22.5% Below Average, the middle 35% Average, the next 22.5% Above Average, and the top 10% High. Morningstar Risk is measured for up to three time periods (3, 5, and 10 years). These separate measures are then weighted and averaged to produce an overall measure for the fund. Funds with less than three years of performance history are not rated.

Multiple Managers

This refers to the arrangement in which two or more people are involved in the fund management, and they manage independently; quite often the fund has divided net assets in set amounts among the individual managers. In most cases, multiple managers are employed at different subadvisors or investment firms.

Mutual Fund

An investment company that sells shares to people and uses the money to buy stocks, bonds, and other investments. The mutual fund passes on the earnings from its investments to its shareholders. Mutual funds are an easy way for individuals to invest in a lot of securities at once.

N

NAV

A fund's net asset value (NAV) represents its per-share price. A fund's NAV is derived by dividing the total net assets of the fund, less fees and expenses, by the number of shares outstanding.

Net Income Growth %

This figure for Morningstar products represents the annualized rate of net-income growth over the trailing one-year period for the stocks held by a fund. Net-income growth gives a good picture of the rate at which companies have grown their profits. All things being equal, stocks with higher net-income growth rates are generally more desirable than those with slower net-income growth rates. Morningstar aggregates net-income growth figures for mutual funds using a median methodology, whereby domestic stocks are ordered from highest to lowest based on their net-income growth rates. One adds up the asset weighting of each holding until the total is equal to or greater than half of the total weighting of all domestic stocks in the fund. The net-income growth rate for that stock is then used to represent the net-income growth rate of the total portfolio.

P

Portfolio

All the investments you own or, similarly, all the investments your fund owns.

Potential Capital-Gains Exposure

The percentage of a fund's total assets that represent capital appreciation. In other words, this is how much of the fund's assets would be subject to taxation if the fund were to liquidate today. Where a negative number appears, the fund has reported losses on its books. This information (realized and unrealized appreciation and net assets) is taken from the fund's annual report. Although funds rarely liquidate their entire portfolio, a fund with a higher potential capital gains exposure may be more likely to realize large capital gains in the event of a manager change or strategy shift. A high capital-gains exposure often accompanies a low turnover strategy, wherein a fund holds stocks over the long term, allowing profits to accumulate.

Price/Book Ratio

The price/book (P/B) ratio of a fund is the weighted average of the price/book ratios of all the stocks in a fund's portfolio. Book value is the total assets of a company, less total liabilities (sometimes referred to as carrying value). A company's price/book value is calculated by dividing the market price of its outstanding stock by the company's book value, and then adjusting for the number of shares outstanding. (Stocks with negative book values are excluded from this calculation.)

Price/Cash-Flow Ratio

This represents the weighted average of the price/cash-flow ratios of the stocks in a fund's portfolio. Price/cash-flow represents the amount an investor is willing to pay for a dollar generated from a particular company's operations. Price/cash-flow shows the ability of a business to generate cash and acts as a gauge of liquidity and solvency. Because accounting conventions differ among nations, reported earnings (and P/E ratios) may not be comparable across national boundaries. Price/cash-flow attempts to provide an internationally standard measure of a firm's stock price relative to its financial performance.

Price/Earnings Ratio

The price/earnings (P/E) ratio of a fund is the weighted average of the price/earnings ratios of the stocks in a fund's portfolio. The P/E ratio of a company, which is a comparison of the cost of the company's stock and its trailing 12-month earnings per share, is calculated by dividing a stock's price by its earnings. In computing the average, Morningstar weights each portfolio holding by the percentage of equity assets it represents, so that larger positions have proportionately greater influence on

the fund's final P/E. A high P/E usually indicates that the market will pay more to obtain the company's earnings because it believes in the firm's ability to increase its earnings. (P/Es can also be artificially inflated if a company has very weak trailing earnings, and thus a very small number in this equation's denominator.) A low P/E indicates the market has less confidence that the company's earnings will increase; however, a fund manager or an individual with a "value investing" approach may believe such stocks have an overlooked or undervalued potential for appreciation.

Price/Sales Ratio

This represents the weighted average of the price/sales ratios of the stocks in a fund's portfolio. Price/sales represents the amount an investor is willing to pay for a dollar generated from a particular company's operations.

Prime-Rate Funds

These funds invest in senior corporate loans and senior secured debt securities. These funds anticipate paying dividends that float or reset at a margin above a generally recognized rate such as LIBOR (London Inter-Bank Offer Rate).

Principal

The money you originally invested. It can also mean the face value of a bond, which you get back when the bond matures. You don't count income or capital gains as principal for an investment, even if you reinvest them.

Projected Earnings Growth %

This figure on Morningstar.com represents the projected one-year earnings growth rate of the stocks held by a fund. Projected earnings growth gives a good picture of a company's growth projects. All things being equal, stocks with better growth prospects are more desirable than those with poorer growth rates. Morningstar aggregates projected earnings growth figures for mutual funds using a median methodology, whereby domestic stocks are ordered from highest to lowest based on their projected earnings growth. One adds up the asset weighting of each holding until the total is equal to or greater than half of the total weighting of all domestic stocks in the fund. The projected earnings growth rate for that stock is then used to represent the projected one-year earnings growth rate of the total portfolio.

Prospectus

A guide legally required by the SEC that explains many of the details about a mutual fund. Always read the prospectus before making an investment. A mutual fund's prospectus will tell you how the fund picks investments, how much it has made in the past, and what its major risks are.

Q

Qualified Access

This is any fund offered through a retirement plan such as an employee pension plan, 401(k), or 403(b) plan. These plans meet the necessary IRS requirements to allow participants to deduct the amount of their investments from their taxable income, thereby investing pretax dollars. Money builds up on a tax-deferred basis, and when the investor withdraws money, both the principal and profit are treated as taxable income.

R

Return

The amount of money your investment made for you. Usually return is given as a percentage of the amount you invested, so a $5,000 investment that made you $400 earned an 8% return ($400 divided by $5,000).

Revenue Growth

This figure represents the rate of revenue growth over the trailing one-year period for the stocks held by a fund. Revenue growth gives a good picture of the rate at which companies have been able to expand their businesses. All things being equal, stocks with higher revenue growth rates are generally more desirable than those with slower revenue growth rates.

Role in Portfolio

Morningstar designates funds as core, supporting player, or specialty. Core funds should be the bulk of an investor's portfolio, while supporting players contribute to a portfolio but are secondary to the core. Specialty offerings tend to be speculative and should typically only be a small portion of investors' portfolios.

R-Squared

The percentage of an investment's returns explained by movements in a benchmark index. An S&P 500 index fund will have an R-squared of nearly 100 compared with the S&P 500 Index, since they move in step, but would have a much lower one compared with a gold index.

S

Sector Fund

A mutual fund that invests in companies in a specific type of business. Sector funds can invest in a general industry, such as technology companies, or a specific industry, such as Internet companies. Because they focus on only one industry, they're usually riskier than general stock funds.

Sector Risk

The danger that the stock of many of the companies in one sector (such as health care or technology) will fall in price at the same time because of an event that affects the entire industry.

Shareholder Report

A guide your mutual fund sends out at least twice per year with information on how the fund is doing and what investments it owns. It usually includes a letter from your fund's president and/or manager.

Sharpe Ratio

This risk-adjusted measure was developed by Nobel Laureate William Sharpe. It is calculated by using standard deviation and excess return to determine reward per unit of risk. The higher the Sharpe ratio, the better the fund's historical risk-adjusted performance. The Sharpe ratio is calculated for the past 36-month period by dividing a fund's annualized excess returns over the risk-free rate by its annualized standard deviation. It is recalculated on a monthly basis. Since this ratio uses standard deviation as its risk measure, it is most appropriately applied when analyzing a fund that is an investor's sole holding. The Sharpe ratio can be used to compare directly how much risk two funds each had to bear to earn excess return over the risk-free rate.

Socially Responsible Funds

These funds, also known as SRI funds, invest according to noneconomic guidelines. Funds may make investments based on such issues as environmental responsibility, human rights, or religious views. For example, socially responsible funds may take a proactive stance by selectively investing in environmentally friendly companies or firms with good employee relations. This group also includes funds that avoid investing in companies involved in promoting alcohol, tobacco, or gambling, or those in the defense industry.

Standard Deviation

This statistical measurement of dispersion about an average, depicts how widely a mutual fund's returns varied over a certain period of time. Investors use the standard deviation of historical performance to try to predict the range of returns that are most likely for a given fund. When a fund has a high standard deviation, the predicted range of performance is wide, implying greater volatility. Standard deviation is most appropriate for measuring the risk of a fund that is an investor's only holding. The figure cannot be combined for more than one fund because the standard deviation for a portfolio of multiple funds is a function of not only the individual standard deviations, but also of the degree of correlation among the funds' returns.

Subadvisor

In some cases, a mutual fund's advisor employs another company, called the subadvisor, to handle the fund's day-to-day management. In these instances, the portfolio manager generally works for the fund's subadvisor, and not the advisor.

T

Target-Retirement Funds

These funds are managed for investors planning to retire—or to begin withdrawing substantial portions of their investments—in a particular year. The funds follow an asset-allocation strategy that grows more conservative as the target date nears.

Taxable Account

An investment account that isn't sheltered from taxes. This means you have to pay taxes on any interest payments or distributions, as well as on any gains you realize when you sell the investment. With tax-deferred accounts, such as IRAs and 401(k)s, you can postpone the payment of these taxes.

Tax-Adjusted Return

These returns are adjusted for taxes and sales charges and follow the SEC guidelines for calculating returns before sale of shares. The tax-adjusted return shows a fund's annualized after-tax total return for the 5- and 10-year periods, excluding any capital-gains effects that would result from selling the fund at the end of the period. To determine this figure, all income and short-term capital-gains distributions are taxed at the maximum federal rate at the time of distribution. Long-term capital gains are taxed at a 20% rate. The after-tax portion is then reinvested in the fund. State and local taxes are ignored, and only the capital-gains are adjusted for tax-exempt funds, as the income from these funds is nontaxable.

Tax-Cost Ratio

This represents the percentage-point reduction in an annualized return that results from income taxes. The calculation assumes investors pay the maximum federal rate on capital gains and ordinary income. For example, if a fund made short-term capital-gains and income distributions that averaged 10% of its NAV over the past three years, an investor in the 35% tax bracket would have a tax-cost ratio of 3.5 percentage points. The 35% tax rate was used for illustrative purposes. However, our tax-cost calculation uses the maximum income-tax rate that applied during the year in which the distribution was made.

Tax-Deferred

An account that lets you wait before paying taxes on your earnings. Your defined contribution account is tax deferred since you only pay taxes on earnings when you withdraw them, not when you earn them. Because more of your money works for you through compounding, tax deferral allows you to earn more.

Tax-Exempt

Off-limits to the Internal Revenue Service. Few investments are completely tax-exempt. Interest from city bonds, for example, is usually free from federal taxes but may be subject to state taxes. Earnings on Roth IRA investments are tax-exempt because you never pay taxes on them.

Tax-Managed Funds

These funds are managed with a sensitivity to tax ramifications. They try to minimize taxable distributions through various methods.

Total Cost Projections

Found in a fund's prospectus, these figures show how much an investor would expect to pay in expenses—sales charges (loads) and fees—over the next 3, 5, and 10 years, assuming a $10,000 investment that grows by 5% per year with redemption at the end of each time period. Total cost projections are commonly based on the past year's incurred fees or an estimate of the current fiscal year's fees, should a portion of the overall fee structure change as of the printing of the fund's most current prospectus. Newer funds are required to print total cost projections for one- and three-year time periods only since longer-term projections may not be possible to estimate.

Total Return

A fund's gain, in percentage terms, over a specified period of time. Total return consists of any income the fund paid out, plus (or minus) any increase (or decrease) in the value of the portfolio's holdings. We assume reinvestment of income and capital-gains distributions in our calculations. Returns are not adjusted for sales charges or redemption fees.

Trailing 12-Month Yield

Yield is the percentage income your portfolio returned over the past 12 months. It is calculated by taking the weighted average of the yields of the stocks and funds that compose the portfolio. Dividend yield for the underlying stocks and funds is calculated by dividing the total dollar amount the security paid out as income to shareholders by the share price. Note that for mutual funds, the dollar-income value includes interest income from fixed-income securities, dividends from stocks, and realized gains from currency transactions.

Turnover Ratio

This is a measure of the fund's trading activity, which is computed by taking the lesser of purchases or sales (excluding all securities with maturities of less than one year) and dividing by average monthly net assets. A turnover ratio of 100% or more does not necessarily suggest that all securities in the portfolio have been traded. In practical terms, the resulting percentage loosely represents the percentage of the portfolio's holdings that have changed over the past year. A low turnover figure (20% to 30%) would indicate a buy-and-hold strategy. High turnover (more than 100%) would indicate an investment strategy involving considerable buying and selling of securities. Morningstar does not calculate turnover ratios. The figure is culled directly from the financial highlights of the fund's annual report.

V

Volatility

Refers to fluctuations in the performance of an investment. A money-market account with a fixed $1 share price has no volatility, but a mutual fund that invests in stocks might be very volatile. In general, investments that generate large returns are more volatile than investments with lower returns.

Y

Yield

The interest or dividends your investments produce. It doesn't include capital gains, which you may receive when you sell an investment. Yield is figured as a percentage of the investment's worth. A $100 bond yielding 5% pays you $5 a year.

Recommended Readings

Common Sense on Mutual Funds: New Imperatives for the Intelligent Investor by John C. Bogle, 2000. Published by John Wiley & Sons. The best book on funds, period.

Classics: An Investor's Anthology by Charles D. Ellis with James R. Vertin, 1990. Published by Business One Irwin.

Asset Allocation: Balancing Financial Risk by Roger C. Gibson, 2000. Published by McGraw-Hill Trade. An essential text that has influenced a whole generation of financial advisors.

The Intelligent Investor: The Definitive Book on Value Investing, Revised Edition by Benjamin Graham, Jason Zweig, 2003. Published by Harper Business. The wisdom in this book still resonates decades after its publication.

Security Analysis: The Classic 1934 Edition by Benjamin Graham and David L. Dodd, 1996. Published by McGraw-Hill Trade. This book is considered by many top managers to be the bible of investing.

Buffett: The Making of an American Capitalist by Roger Lowenstein, 1996. Published by Main Street Books. A great biography. You cannot call yourself a serious investor and not be a student of Buffett.

One Up on Wall Street: How to Use What You Already Know to Make Money in the Market by Peter Lynch, 2000. Published by Simon & Schuster. This classic is one of the most accessible books on picking individual stocks.

A Random Walk Down Wall Street by Burton G. Malkiel, 2004. Published by WW Norton & Company. Makes the case for indexing and shows how much of what we attribute as brilliance among managers may really be random chance.

The Wall Street Journal Guide to Understanding Money and Investing by Kenneth M. Morris, Virginia B. Morris, and Alan M. Siegel, 2004. Published by Fireside. This user-friendly guide provides novices with solid money and market information.

continued...

The New Commonsense Guide to Mutual Funds by Mary Rowland, 1998. Published by Bloomberg Press. Rowland's guide is the perfect choice if you would rather not spend a lot of time reading about funds—or want to read about them in short, digestible chunks.

The Money Game by Adam Smith, 1976. Published by Vintage. While the attitudes are dated, this remains a great history.

The Only Investment Guide You'll Ever Need by Andrew Tobias, 2002. Published by Harvest Books. A great introduction to thinking about the key trade-offs of personal finance.

The Money Masters and the New Money Masters by John Train, 1994. Published by HarperBusiness. Wonderful introductions to some of the best money managers ever.

Additional Morningstar Resources

In addition to this workbook, Morningstar publishes a number of products about mutual funds. There's something for everyone, from newsletters to sourcebooks. Most can be found at your local library, or by calling Morningstar to start your own subscriptions (866-608-9570).

Morningstar® Mutual Funds™

This twice-monthly report service features full-page financial reports and analysis of 1,600 funds specially selected for building and maintaining balanced portfolios. Our report service is favored by professionals and serious investors and carried in more than 4,000 libraries nationwide. Trial subscriptions are available.

Morningstar® FundInvestor™

Monthly newsletter offers 48 pages of fund investing help—including Morningstar model portfolios, analysis of funds, funds to avoid, the FundInvestor 500, and Morningstar Analyst Picks.

Morningstar.com

Our Web site features investing information on funds, stocks, bonds, retirement planning, and more. In addition to powerful portfolio tools, you'll find daily articles by Morningstar analysts and editors. Much information on the site is free, and there's a reasonably priced Premium Membership service for investors requiring more in-depth information and sophisticated analytical tools.

Morningstar® Funds 500™

Annual book of full-page reports on 500 selected funds. The new edition appears in January of each year and includes complete year-end results of funds covered, as well as general fund industry performance information.

Morningstar Guide to Mutual Funds

5-Star Strategies for Success

Here's the perfect desktop resource for new and experienced investors. Encapsulating 20 years of experience analyzing funds, it shows you what works in fund investing. In addition to plain-English chapters on key topics, it includes real-world examples and 14 investor checklists. Hardbound, 6"x 9", 286 pages.

Answer Key

Quiz 101: What is a Mutual Fund?

1 c. Mutual funds are corporations under the Investment Company Act of
       1940 and are regulated by the SEC, but, unlike a bank account, they are
       not insured against loss.

2 b. NAV, or net asset value, is calculated by dividing a fund's total assets
       by the number of shares, giving you the price per share.

3 c. As a shareholder, you are an owner of the fund. Fidelity runs
       Magellan on behalf of the fund's shareholders, and its board of directors
       represents the interests of the shareholders.

4 b. Mutual funds are regulated by the Securities and Exchange Commission,
       but they are not insured or guaranteed.

5 b. When you sell your fund shares, you receive cash in return.

Quiz 102: Mutual Funds and NAVs

1 c. To arrive at a fund's NAV, divide its total assets by the number of
       shares outstanding. ($10 million in securities + $2 million in cash)/
       1 million shares.

2 c. Mutual funds calculate their NAVs once each day, at the market's
       close. So if you buy a fund during the day, your purchase price is based
       on the fund's NAV at the end of that day.

3 a. A fund's number of shares outstanding fluctuates when investors buy or
       sell the fund. These purchases or sales have no effect on the fund's
       NAV because the only thing that affects NAV is the performance of the
       fund's underlying portfolio holdings.

4 c. Because funds issue fractional shares, either Fund A or Fund B would be available to an investor with just $100 in hand; $100 would buy 10 shares of Fund A or .909 shares of Fund B.

Quiz 103: Understanding Total Return

1 c. Total return includes all the elements of return, both income and capital gains that have been realized and distributed, as well as any unrealized gains in the fund's underlying portfolio, which are reflected in NAV changes.

2 b. NAV slips once a distribution is made. Remember, though, shareholders still have their money—they simply now have some in the fund and some in cash.

3 a. While a fund's total return includes any income distributions made over the past 12 months, it also reflects any capital-gains distributions and NAV changes. Yield, meanwhile, measures income distributions only.

4 b. Shareholders elect whether they want to take their distributions in cash or whether they want them reinvested, or put back, in the fund to continue to grow.

5 c. When funds make distributions, you are none the poorer. Because you have chosen to reinvest, your distribution of $50 ($5 x 10 shares) buys 10 more shares at the new $5 NAV. You now have a total of 20 shares in the fund.

Quiz 104: Fund Costs

1 b. Annual expenses cover managing and administering the fund, as well as marketing and brokerage expenses. Only certain funds charge redemption fees. Some fund families charge account-maintenance fees if your account value falls below a set amount.

2   c.   If you're buying shares with front-end loads, you pay when you buy the fund. If you're buying shares with back-end loads, you pay when you sell the fund. If you're buying level-load shares, you pay a little bit each year.

3   a.   Not all funds charge 12b-1 fees, but if they do, that cost is in the expense ratio. The expense ratio does not include the costs of buying and selling securities (or brokerage fees), nor any borrowing costs (or interest expense).

4   c.   The less the fund charges, the more you get to keep, and the better your returns tend to be.

5   a.   You should pay less for fund types with a narrow range of returns, such as bond or large-cap stock funds. Look for funds with expense ratios of 1% or less. The range of returns is wider for small-cap or foreign funds, so you should expect to pay more.

Quiz 105: Mutual Funds and Taxes

1   b.   You have some control over your taxes by buying and selling a fund, but fund managers decide when to buy and sell securities for the fund. They decide when to realize gains and make distributions. Fund shareholders have no control over those decisions.

2   a.   Even if you reinvest your distributions, you still have to pay taxes on the distributions. Moreover, funds that lose money in one year can pay out taxable distributions—remember our technology funds example?

3   c.   Funds that own income-producing securities, such as bonds, pay out lots of income and therefore aren't remarkably tax-efficient. Stock funds with ultralow turnovers of 10% or less tend to be tax-friendly.

4   a.   If you buy a fund just before it makes a distribution, you'll pay taxes on that distribution, even though you haven't enjoyed any of the appreciation that led to that distribution.

5 c. If you're investing in a taxable account, it's wise to consider taxes when investing. However, don't let the tax tail wag the investment dog. What's most important is how much you keep after taxes, not how much Uncle Sam gets.

Quiz 106: Important Fund Documents

1 c. All prospectuses include information about management fees. If funds have a team of managers working on the fund, they do not currently have to list all team members. The names of the board of directors typically appear in the Statement of Additional Information.

2 a. The Investment Objective section details if the fund seeks long-term growth or income, for example. To find out what types of securities the fund invests in, go to the Strategy section. The Risk section describes the risks particular to the fund.

3 b. The prospectus provides a view of all fund costs, including management and operational fees, as well as any commissions. The SAI breaks down those costs into their components.

4 b. Your manager runs the fund day to day so you are most likely to find useful context in that letter. The president's letter tends to focus on economic and market trends. The footnotes provide portfolio details.

5 a. Stocks are listed in the Portfolio Holdings section while an expense breakdown appears in the Statement of Operations. The Per-Share Data features a series of ratios such as annual expenses and turnover as well as per-share distribution and NAVs.

Quiz 107: How to Purchase a Fund

1 b. Advisors can charge you a fee or get a commission from products, such as mutual funds, that they sell. They can also charge a combination of fees and commissions. They cannot, however, take a portion of the fund manager's fee.

2 c. Loads are commissions that are paid to advisors. Fund managers receive a portion of the fund's management fee.

3 a. There's just no reason to pay a load if you are not receiving financial advice. Either buy no-load funds directly through fund families, or invest through a no-transaction fee network (or fund supermarket).

4 c. There are no up-front costs with a no-transaction fee network. The networks charge funds for being included, and funds very often pass along these charges to all shareholders (whether or not they invest via a supermarket) in their expense ratios.

5 a. Investing all in one place makes record keeping easier and makes moving to and from funds a snap, too. And as long as you stick with one of the largest fund families, you'll have plenty of diversification options, too.

Quiz 108: Methods for Investing in Mutual Funds

1 b. Because stocks go up more often than they go down and because of the effects of compounding, market-timers can't just get their calls right half the time and outperform. They must be right two-thirds of the time. That's a lot.

2 b. With a lump-sum investment, you would have purchased the most shares at the lowest NAV—right at the beginning of the period.

3 c. The dollar-cost-averaging investor has probably accumulated more shares than the timer or the lump-sum investor and had some cash on hand when the lump-sum investor was losing money.

4 a. In a rising market, a lump-sum investor will earn more than someone who is dollar-cost averaging into a fund. However, dollar-cost averaging limits risk, instills discipline, and often allows investors to get into high-minimum funds for less.

5 c. You would want to invest as much as you can now because the market
       is more likely to go up than down over the next 10 years. But
       we would recommend investing a little each month or each quarter, as
       well, so that you remain disciplined.

Quiz 109: Five Questions to Ask Before Buying a Mutual Fund

1 b. Analyzing returns in isolation does not provide a context in which to
       evaluate a fund's performance fairly. Instead, compare a fund
       to an index or a group of funds that buy the same types of securities.

2 a. In general, the greater the return on investment, the greater the
       potential for loss. Although Fund A is a higher returning fund, some
       investors might find it too volatile.

3 b. Consult the fund's portfolio and portfolio statistics, such as the
       Morningstar style box, to figure out how the manager invests. Compare
       a fund with a benchmark to see how competitive it has been.

4 c. The fund manager chooses investments for you. While the manager
       may practice a certain style that's common at the fund company
       he or she works for, the manager is the one choosing the individual
       securities.

5 b. You can't control the whims of the market—or the whims of your fund
       manager. You can only control the types of funds you own and how
       they fit together.

Quiz 110: Why Knowing Your Fund Manager Matters

1 b. Team-managed funds use two or more people who work together.
       Single-manager funds use one lead manager with others pitching in
       with research and training. Multiple-manager funds are quite rare.

2 a. Because index funds are passively managed—in other words, their managers aren't actively choosing which securities to buy or sell—manager changes don't matter much.

3 c. If a fund lists only one fund manager and that manager leaves, the fund may be poised for change. If only one member leaves from a team, in contrast, there should be some continuity in the fund's performance.

4 b. While star managers may seem alluring, be sure that there's some back-up or bench strength in the family. Why? Because managers who do well at mediocre families eventually move on.

5 c. If the fund was team-managed or if the family has other skilled managers on staff, staying the course isn't a bad idea. If it's an index fund or a fund from a category with a modest range of returns, there's probably no reason to sell at all.

Quiz 111: Your First Fund

1 c. Your first fund should be one that owns a significant number of stocks from a variety of industries.

2 b. Funds that own large companies, in general, may not necessarily be higher returning or cheaper, but they tend to be steadier investments than those owning smaller companies.

3 b. Blend funds own stocks with value and growth characteristics and typically don't favor particular sectors over others. They therefore offer more diversification than most large-value or large-growth funds do.

4 a. Funds focusing on only one area of the market are not necessarily poor performers or more expensive, but they tend to be less stable than funds owning stocks from various industries.

5 c. Most of the big fund families are reliable and offer a wide range of solid funds—but they aren't always chart toppers.

Quiz 112: What to Look For

1 b. **Index-fund managers are passive investors: They buy what an index does. What they like or don't like doesn't factor in to what gets bought or sold.**

2 c. **Index funds are generally low cost and predictable. Index-fund managers don't pick stocks in the traditional sense, though.**

3 c. **A fund of funds literally owns other mutual funds. Those funds may own stocks, bonds, or both.**

4 a. **Funds of funds usually offer access to lots of other funds for a low minimum; they also limit paperwork. But a fund of funds can have high hidden costs, charging shareholders expenses on top of the expenses of the funds it owns.**

5 b. **All life-cycle funds try to offer investors of a certain age or risk tolerance a one-stop shop. Some are indexed while others are actively managed.**

Also in the Morningstar Fearless Investing Series

Diversify Your Fund Portfolio
Our intermediate-level workbook explains and illustrates how to build a profitable portfolio of mutual funds.

Maximize Your Fund Returns
In this advance-level workbook, you'll learn how to rebalance your portfolio, calculate your personal rate of return, and more.

Coming in Summer 2005—Morningstar Fearless Investing Series for Stocks